Entry Without Inspection

SERIES EDITORS

Valerie Boyd
John Griswold

SERIES ADVISORY BOARD

Dan Gunn
Pam Houston
Phillip Lopate
Dinty W. Moore
Lia Purpura
Patricia Smith
Ned Stuckey-French

Entry Without Inspection

A Writer's Life in El Norte

CECILE PINEDA

THE UNIVERSITY OF GEORGIA PRESS
ATHENS

© 2020 by the University of Georgia Press
Athens, Georgia 30602
www.ugapress.org
All rights reserved
Designed by Kaelin Chappell Broaddus
Set in 9.75/13.5 Dolly Pro by Kaelin Chappell Broaddus

Most University of Georgia Press titles are
available from popular e-book vendors.

Printed digitally

Library of Congress Cataloging-in-Publication Data

Names: Pineda, Cecile, author.
Title: Entry without inspection : a writer's life in El Norte /
   Cecile Pineda.
Description: Athens : The University of Georgia Press, [2020] |
   Series: Crux : the Georgia series in literary nonfiction
Identifiers: LCCN 2020022314 | ISBN 9780820358468 (paperback) |
   ISBN 9780820358475 (ebook)
Subjects: LCSH: Pineda, Cecile. | Women authors, American—20th
   century—Biography. | Authors, American—20th century—
   Biography.
Classification: LCC PS3566.I5214 Z46 2020 | DDC 818/.5403 [B]—dc23
LC record available at https://lccn.loc.gov/2020022314

For Michael and Shelley

*Two truths approach each other.
One comes from within,
one comes from without—
and where they meet you have the chance
to catch a look at yourself.*

—TOMAS TRANSTRÖMER

If a man will not work, he shall not eat.

—THESSALONIANS 3:10

CONTENTS

Preface xi

I. QUESTIONS

                Prologue 3

1. Secrets 5

                Day One 14

2. Screen Doors 20

                Day Two 24

3. Freedom 29

                Day Three 41

II. THE WAY TO ART

4. Divorcing Mom and Dad 45
5. Marking Time: Bottle Washer 51
6. Chief Cook 57

                Day Four 61

7. San Francisco Story   69
          Day Five   69
8. Strike   79
          Day Six   80
9. Theatre of Man   88
10. Invitation to a Threesomes   109
          Day Seven   115
11. Zigzagging with Goya   126

III. MAKING WORDS

12. Consultation with a Sibyl   133
13. Writing with the Body   144
          Day Eight   147

IV. GETTING TO THE ROOT OF THINGS

14. Through the Looking Glass   153
          Day Nine   157
15. Facing It   159
16. Summoning the Diamond Boss   168
          Day Ten   175
17. Last Things   177

Acknowledgments   189
Appendix. Jean Blum: Finger in Goliath's Eye   191
About the Author   221

PREFACE

The reader will find between these pages a strange approximation of a life narrative punctuated by ten Days, ten initially unexplained, apparently random interludes, which intercut the main narrative like a palimpsest of sorts, because *Entry Without Inspection* is more than just a memoir. My early life took me from explorations in the experimental theater of the sixties and seventies into the life of a critically acclaimed Chicana writer, the first, with the publication of *Face* by Viking in 1985, to be recognized by the mainstream press. My work drew on the politics of my host country, my preoccupations with nuclear proliferation, with the global culture rooted in my readings over a lifetime, and more recently, with the danger of climate collapse threatening humanity at large.

With progress through these pages, the reader may begin to suspect that the connection between the life and the Days is far from arbitrary as they join at the memoir's conclusion because *Entry Without Inspection* is the story of a life in search of itself, stamped by an absence, an absence for many years without name, the name of family separation, of which we have become all too aware in 2019 with the depredations of our current white supremacist, racist regime.

Cecile Pineda
Berkeley, California
November 6, 2019

Entry Without Inspection

I

Questions

1
Questions

Prologue

News photographs showed her to be an elderly, diminutive woman of no particularly distinctive appearance, a woman one could imagine knitting, a small cat curled in her lap. It was that very ordinariness that drew my interest, for Jean Blum was the first whistleblower to expose a death in immigrant detention. Her discovery of that first "disappearance" prompted a *New York Times* investigation that revealed that by 2009, within the seven years since ICE was first established, at least 106 deaths had already occurred in the jails operated by Homeland Security under the auspices of its Immigrant and Customs Enforcement arm.

I needed to find out what prompted Jean Blum at age seventy-five to break from an unremarkable life to come to the aid of people apparently so unlike herself. I did something I had never done before. I took a plane to New Jersey. Over some ten days I listened to her story until my notes took up a full journal. Those ten days are reflected in the ten Days appearing here. I discovered she had been a Holocaust survivor. And yes, she was an accomplished knitter, but she kept dogs, not cats.

Quite unaware, I had begun to write the words that would overlay the story of my true beginnings, one I had not yet unraveled. In the writing, I would bring together two apparently disconnected life stories, one laid down in my early adulthood and one emerging much later in life. That latter could be seen as an improvisation by someone whose story until now has been a search for identity, a theme reflected in my voice-switching fiction, a story that in the drafting cannot be traced so much in determined lines as in a series of hatch marks, which, taken together, only reveal their true pattern over time. They are words written by someone whose family ties were severed long ago and whose culture was cast aside at the U.S.-Mexican border when my father fled his country at the age of sixteen in 1910 and entered the United States under an assumed name, an extralegal immigration referred to by ICE as "entry without inspection."

In those ten days, I began uncovering the pattern of U.S. immigration policy, a story that reverts to the year before my father married my mother in 1931.

1. Secrets

Both my parents were well past their prime when I was born—my mother, French speaking, born in Switzerland in 1888; my father, Harvard graduate and polyglot, born in Mexico City in 1894. If I was not the boy my father's macho culture favored, neither was I my mother's ideal—a Dresden-white-skinned, blue-eyed replica of her younger sister, Blanche, which in French means "white," who was dead of diphtheria at the age of twelve.

Although my parents were clueless about raising children, they chose as my godmother (fig. 1) one of their friends who, though she was French, gave me my first introduction to Mexico, one I would never forget. When my mother first took me to visit Mayenne, my childhood name for her, I must have been four years old. I still remember the smell of straw given off by her huge hamper baskets and all the little donkeys with sombrero-wearing riders, each one woven in combinations of different Crayola colors—red, purple, magenta, yellow, and green. Laid out on her dining table were shiny bright yellow, orange, green, and red papier-mâché fruits and vegetables and a set of Oaxaca ware the color of squashed caterpillars. How I wanted to smell everything and touch all the bright and shining surfaces, but my mother warned me if I touched anything, it might break.

Like many children of immigrants, especially of my generation, I derived little sense from where I came or who my people re-

FIG. 1. Jane. E. Browne, my godmother, "Mayenne."

ally were. When I began publishing fiction in my fifties, I was invited to write about my art. The title, "Deracinated: The Writer Re-invents Her Sources" (published in *Máscaras*, edited by Lucha Corpi, by Third Woman Press in 1997), might as well have read: "By Writing, the Writer Invents Herself." At least with my debut novel I had reclaimed my name, the one I was born with. Shortly after I published *Frieze*, a novel set in ninth-century India and Java, a Mexican scholar reproved me: "Why couldn't you have written about a Mexican pyramid?"

But I had visited a pyramid outside Yogyakarta in Indonesia, nowhere near Mexico. "You have to have a world before you can put things in it," the fictional father of *Fishlight* says, something my Mexican father could never understand.

I first became conscious of the pain I felt for the history that had been denied me when, shortly after the publication of *The Love Queen of the Amazon*, MANA, the Washington-based Mexican American Women's National Association, invited me to speak. In my talk, I mentioned that some of the stories I'd included in that book were inspired by my father's fabrications, but at a certain point, I broke down, unable to continue. In the presence of an audience composed of women whose histories were apparently available to them, I mourned the absence of my own.

It has taken me a lifetime to uncover my past, to find the roots that make me what I am—a person whose living, whose thoughts and actions, though they seem to announce themselves publicly, are forged in solitude—and to search my past for what it might mean to be born, an only child, to people who set up an image of family no more convincing than a cardboard cutout in a druggist's window.

The New York world I was born into was unlike the present one. Not many people owned cars. There were no talking gas pumps that told you what to buy. Seven-story-tall signs screaming ExxonMobil or McDonalds hadn't been invented. Along the shoulders of two-lane U.S. highways, Burma-Shave reminders popped up every fifty yards. We shopped at what we now dismiss as "mom-and-pop" stores: a few shelves displaying Campbell's chicken noodle soup and Heinz Boston baked beans, a few planks mounted on sawhorses displaying truck-farm vegetables. Butcher shops with sawdust on the floor, where the cleaver drummed steadily against the block, shops where fish was poor folk's fare because abundance coupled with lack of demand brought it home cheap and wrapped in newspaper. A world where chunks of butter were carved out from wooden tubs and slapped onto parchment paper as you watched the scale's red needle swing its arc, anxious that you still had money left to pay for it.

It was a quieter world, one inhabited by only half the people living in it now. The newsreel voices of film and radio shrilled their mythologies, and if television had not yet reduced politics to dog and pony shows, the message was the same: America was Number One, Always Right, White, and Protestant. And, Depression notwithstanding, things were never greater or better or more prosperous, and in the meantime, there was peace.

There was no separate (but equal) messaging for the northern ghettoes or for sharecroppers down South or for miners in Appalachia or for the Germans and Poles stoking the Midwest's Bessemer furnaces. But so-called minorities (usually nonwhite, non-Episcopalian folks) had some things going for them most white people had left behind: a commonly held past, a sense of their origins, and a feeling of belonging, some of it based on the very marginalization that worked to keep them down. Forced to keep to themselves, they still had each other, and handed down through generations, they still had stories to tell and music and dances and home recipes that bound them together. All the black people—the people we lived with—had jazz. They had gospel, that old-time religion to sustain them through the slavery and lynching years. Appalachia had a centuries-long history of folk song and resistance. Workingmen had labor songs, and they knew them by heart. And Mexicans? At that time almost no Mexicans lived in New York. They gravitated to California and Texas, to the heat and dust and soaring temperatures of the dirt rows where they stooped year after year, migrants moving from crop to crop, putting food on the nation's table—the lowest-paid, least organized, and most despised workers in America. But the story of my own Mexican father was quite different. Trained at Harvard as a linguist, he taught Spanish at New York's City College in the midst of the Depression.

From the start, it was language that threw me a lifeline. Given my surname, it ought to have been Spanish, yet because my Swiss French mother was unwilling to learn Spanish, when my father agreed we'd speak French at home, French became the language that lent my early life its shape.

We lived in a six-story Manhattan apartment house, eight apartments to each floor. The front gave on the street. In back a tangle of wash lines gave on the limbo space overlooking the backs of other six-story buildings along the neighboring street. Within each building was a central courtyard. Poverty was all around us, and poverty visited our courtyard.

> Where we lived, the corridors were long and twisty, and the doors on every floor had letters and numbers mixed up on them. There was a big brick courtyard way inside, where nobody could see it from the street. In the winter afternoons, old men would come in ragged coats and mashed in hats. Way down in the courtyard, you could hear their footsteps shuffle in the dust.

One scratched away at an old violin; one even blew a smashed up horn, but most of them just sang songs about mountains, or rivers, or maybe even lakes, places they came from, or places they lost, or maybe the places lost them, and when they finished, you could hear a hush come over the courtyard. Then people slid their windows open and started throwing money out. Sometimes they wrapped the money in little bits of paper so the man down there could get it where it fell, but other times you could hear the pennies bouncing and rolling all over the ground, and the man would have to stoop and bend down to look for them.

The singer would bow and tip his hat and he would say thank you over and over till he made sure he thanked all the ladies that threw him all the pennies, and then his footsteps went away and you couldn't hear them anymore because they got all sucked up inside the basement corridors.

This passage from *Fishlight*, a book that made mythology of my childhood as a five-year-old, tells the bitter truth. But the truth gets transformed into a child's preoccupation with god.

Summertime when the air got hot, my mother let me stay up late and look out the window. In the courtyard people opened up their windows wide. The air simmered like soup, and all the noises got mixed up inside it, all the barking of dogs and the mewing of cats and all the people saying things. When it got dark where you couldn't tell color anymore, you could see people taking off their underwear before they got in bed....

I used to think for God time must be like our courtyard in summertime when the air got so sticky it forgot to breathe, and the heat climbed higher and higher until each floor shimmered like a mirror and you could hear people coughing, or laughing, or crying sometimes, or saying things in other languages, or the fat man next door drawing up gobs of spit behind his half-closed blinds, or the boys playing hide and seek because they couldn't play hockey in the street after it got dark. And my mother screaming and screaming till her hair got on fire and made like it was burning up, and Alice Walsh who sang Rossini in her high, sweet voice while she stood all soapy in the tub, and how her brother said he'd beat me up if I told on her because even in the tub, his sister always had clothes on when she sang, and the parrot from the Amazon who lived somewhere downstairs and who practiced with her every morning, and when she was done, went on hiccoughing to himself, and even the prayers I kept whispering to God every night to make me have blue eyes and long blond hair like they had in fairy tales—all the sounds through the open windows of summer when the air got too hot, too lazy to spread them very far so they all got stuck in there long after they happened—all those noises were not even a whisper in the courtyard of God who had to listen to everything at once.

I was born to a contrary world, a world of people old enough to be my grandparents who, because they were beyond normal childbearing years would have only one of me. From shortly after my birth, they shared no more intimacy; their cultures separated them from each other—and from the great American melting pot.

My mother seems almost never to have been present in these early family scenes, barely content to let me grasp a distantly extended finger. Photographs show my father as the one to cosset me (fig. 2). From before I remember, he became my Pygmalion. I learned to depend on him for any companionship I might enjoy. As my first mentor, he exposed me to a world of wonders: geological exhibits, dinosaur skeletons, and laboratory frogs; he took me to concerts and lectures where he taught me to sit still. He indulged his obsession for fresh air and learning, no matter how harsh the weather, through the peripeteia of long walks, when he talked to me about language and how the same words resurfaced in slightly different form from one language to another. Above all else, he tried to calm my anxieties and rationalize my fears. "Relax," he would say, but his words did nothing to allay my unease.

I must have been three or four the day he bundled me up for a long walk on Riverside Drive. It was the year the Hudson River froze over. You could hear the ice floes rubbing up against each other in the

FIG. 2. "My father was the one to cosset me." Emilio R. Pineda.

river, groaning and yawning like people turning over in their sleep. Snow was lying in sooty lumps on the ground, leftovers from the last storm. We got to a place where lots of people stood whispering. My father slipped a photo negative from his breast pocket. He told me to hold it up to my eyes so that if I looked through it like all the whispering people were doing, I could see the sun.

"Papa Soleil is going to hide behind Mama Moona," he said.

We stood there side by side watching. At first the sun shone bright, but slowly as it seemed to vanish behind the moon, colors disappeared, the birds grew quiet, and the world turned dark. All over there was a scary kind of night. Then there was a sharp burst of light, and very slowly the sun played its game of hide-and-seek until it grew bright again and the birds woke up and remembered it was time to sing.

When I reached up to give him back the negative, nobody was there. I couldn't tell which way was home. I didn't know exactly how we got there, but I didn't cry because by then all the whispering people had gone away and there was nobody to hear me. And then, all of a sudden, my father was there again—as if he hadn't ever disappeared.

I asked him why he did that.

"Did what?"

"Why you disappear like that?"

I could see his jaw working. "Because," he said, "I had to see what you would do." He took me by the hand and we went home.

Although I saw first light in Harlem, by the time I began remembering, we had moved to Morningside Heights, the site of an eponymous battle of the Revolutionary War, a neighborhood where most folks hailed from County Cork. My parochial schoolmates still knew how to dance a jig. In the morning when my mother took me grocery shopping along Amsterdam Avenue's cobblestones, she hustled me past the already boozy voices of the barflies drifting from the Shamrock Bar's open door. Sometimes she stopped to greet someone midway down the block. I liked to dawdle behind her, eavesdropping on our Irish neighbors trading the time of day. *Now wouldn't you know.... Nothin' like it.... I'm after giving him a piece of me mind.... Now you wouldn't be thinkin'...? Oh, dearie...*

"Don't you know listening's impolite?" My mother hurried me along on her way to the German bakery, where she bought semmel to make bread soup. It was the cheapest soup she knew to make.

My mother (fig. 3) took part in my life only when we went shopping. I remember the day—I must have been four—when we had to go downtown, not to buy shoes. My mother wouldn't tell me why. "Wait and see. It's a surprise."

Although children mostly accept things at face value, there was much about my childhood that seemed strange.

FIG. 3. "My mother took part in my life only when we went shopping." Marthe-Alice Pineda and the author holding "Marie Louise."

We got to this place where there was a park on one side and you could see all the people ice skating and spinning on the ice, but my mother didn't want to stop. We went past big gray houses with Christmas trees all lit up in the windows.

"Why don't the lights blink on and off the way ours do?"

"Because the people here are refined and they don't like their lights to blink," my mother said.

We came to a gray house. The front door was glass and it had all black iron bars with all black curlicues. You could see inside to another door that had lace curtains on it. My mother rang the bell. We were standing in the doorway. It was warm there and you couldn't feel the wind.

"What are we waiting for?"

"For Gibby."

The door opened and there was someone tall and skinny with a fluffy pink angora sweater on and little pearls stuck in her ears.

"Mademoiselle!" She threw her arms around my mother. "Maddy's here," she called to somebody upstairs. "Oh, Maddy, dear, we've been expecting you!"

I never heard of Gibby before and she called my mother Maddy like she was someone else. I got this funny feeling in my stomach all of a sudden like we were in the elevator only I got off on the wrong [floor. Except] it was the [right] floor. Everything looked the same, only you could tell it was all different.

Day One

I learned from Jean Blum's archives the depths to which cruelty could sink, but it was not so much the issue of incarceration or even the plight of the immigrants she helped that first drew me to her story. It was her background: she was a Jewish woman, a survivor of the Holocaust.

Jean was born in Warsaw in 1936, an only child. Her father was an electrical engineer. The Polish government charged him and an engineering colleague with designing and overseeing the installation of the national telephone and telegraph communication system. In the first week of September 1939, after the first German bombs fell on Warsaw, her father received a phone call in the middle of the night from the Office of the President of Poland ordering him and his colleague to show up at the bus depot at 6:00 a.m. with their wives, their children, and one suitcase for each family. They were allowed to escape, not because the Poles were particularly concerned for the family as endangered Jews, but because her father possessed the information they needed to deactivate the system he and his colleague had designed to prevent its falling into German hands.

After conducting the two engineers to Romania, where they were debriefed, the Polish officials left them to shift for themselves. Stranded in Romania, Jean's father began making the rounds of all the embassies in Bucharest, searching for a country willing to take them—to no avail. Finally, through their embassy, the French government made him a deal: if he agreed to join the French forces, Jean and her mother would be permitted to travel to Nice, where they would be allowed to stay through the duration of the war. Her father, however, would fight with the French. But after the fall of the collaborationist Vichy government, he was captured by the Germans. He was sent to a prisoner-of-war camp, where his status allowed him to escape the almost certain extermination that awaited most European Jews in the death camps.

As the threat to her life came closer, Jean's mother placed her in an orphanage, but when at war's end her mother came to claim her, so much time had elapsed that Jean failed to recognize her. Reunited after the war, Jean Blum and her family could only be admitted to the United States through congressional intervention. They found themselves living on the fifth floor of a roach-infested Bronx walkup apartment. Her father had to scramble to find employment. He eventually found work as the employee of a brother who owned a record company. Her mother found work as a fabric picker. Left at home alone and overwhelmed by having to adjust to a new school where she spoke no English, Jean wept. One day her father came across Margaret Bourke-White's photographs of the concentration camps taken at the time of the liberation. He cut them out of *Life* magazine and taped them to the wall of her bedroom. "These are the people who have something to cry about," he told her. "Nothing happened to you."

For a lifetime I have resisted returning to these early years because they stir up unnamed fears and memories of relentless punishment, though, whatever their reasons, my parents' cruelty may have had very little to do with me, an insight that would come to me only in adulthood.

Either because they had been unprepared for child-rearing or because they lacked any of its skills, nothing in our apartment was childproof. As a toddler, I took special interest in my mother's travel alarm, which was just within reach where it sat on the coffee table. I grasped it in one pudgy hand to explore the levers on its back casing, and just as I began moving them up and down, a winding screw fell out with a clatter and bounced along the table before it came to rest.

My mother grabbed me. "Emilio," she shouted. My father came to her rescue. He held me while she hit.

Soon after my parents' regular routine of punishment began, they invented what they called The Treatment. They dragged me kicking and resisting along our winding corridor, hitting all the way, pushed me outside, and slammed the door behind me. No matter how hard I clamored to be allowed back in, the hollow metal door stayed shut. After a while, I heard my mother's voice warning the more racket I made, the longer I'd have to keep the doormat company. She wanted me to say I was sorry. My reply wasn't loud enough, maybe because I was crying. She claimed she couldn't hear. I needed to say it louder.

The Treatment became a thing of habit, until one day it stopped as suddenly as it had started. Out on the doormat once more, I stopped crying long enough to notice the small hexagonal tiles paving the entire length of the hallway into the far corner, where the dark doorways disappeared in the obscurity. Along that hallway, each apartment had the same hollow metal door, and alongside each door was a bell I was just tall enough to reach.

When our neighbor, Madame D'Eau, opened her door to me that day, she didn't seem surprised to see me standing there. She asked me to come in. She was an old lady with hair that burst around her head like a dandelion gone to seed. Snow White, her black dog, wiggled his fat old butt, so overjoyed to see me he nearly knocked me over. "Allez, allez," she said. She made him run along so he wouldn't bother me.

Madame D'Eau let me touch everything I wanted, and there were lots of things to touch: an old doll with a porcelain-pink face and hands and feet, and cloth underwear, and a tiny high chair to sit her in. Wooden shoes hung on the wall, one pair big enough for someone big like Madame D'Eau and one for someone small. There was even a miniature pair, not much bigger than a walnut. When I asked her what the littlest ones were for, she took them off their hook and gave them to me. "For me?" She nodded. "If you want." I wanted. I wanted to hug Madame D'Eau. I wanted to live with her and her two cats and her two dogs forever, especially Snow White.

She took me by the hand. "Come, we're going to visit my geranium." She told me how she had to balance it far out on the kitchen windowsill so its bright red flower would catch the courtyard sun. Next to it was a pot in which she was sprouting a fat avocado seed, and from inside its dark crevice I could see a tiny pale green shoot. She promised she'd plant another one for me just as soon as she could polish off another alligator pear.

"Would you like something to eat?"

I nodded. She put three telephone books on a chair, sat me down at her kitchen table, and tucked a huge white napkin around my neck. She took a stout ladle off its hook and poured soup into the bowl she set before me. She showed me how to spoon it slowly from the edge so it wouldn't burn my tongue.

When it was time to go back home, she took me by the hand. We crossed the hall and rang the bell. My mother let me in. She didn't say anything, as if nothing in the world had happened. Madame D'Eau said goodbye, and The Treatment stopped.

Before she married my father, my mother was supposed to have been the belle of the party, but by the time I came into her life, I knew only the humorless, blank face of a deeply discontented woman. It was she who ran the household, produced meals at strictly regular hours, swept the dust bunnies from under the kitchen sink (when she remembered), and, muttering her dark resentments, washed the clothes till her knuckles bled. We ate in the kitchen at a pea-green utility table, where she pronounced a kind of grace: "He who does not work shall not eat."

Saturday mornings when the weather turned balmy, my father took me walking along 125th Street past Blumstein's Jewelry Store, where I loved comparing all the shiny wedding rings displayed in the window on their little velvet cushions. We went past the Apollo Theater all the way to Lexington. We passed girls walking arm in arm and ladies wearing hats with shiny papier-mâché cherries on them. On some street corners, musicians blew the horn. Every time I asked my father to give me a nickel to drop in the hat, they stopped playing just long enough to smile a big "Hi, Sugar, how ya doin'?"

My father never called me Sugar. He had other things in mind. Just past the New York Central Station there was a place we stopped. Inside it was dark except for all the light bulbs and the rows of clay pigeons chugchugchugging along the tracks. "Three shots for two bits," the proprietor said. My father spun two shiny quarters on the glass counter. The man produced a stool high enough for me to stand on. He handed my father a rifle. My father steadied my left hand on the barrel and mashed my finger against the trigger. *Blam!* The recoil always knocked me down. He kept trying to get me to shoot straight, but after a while we didn't go there anymore because he said crying and shooting didn't mix.

When my father sat still thinking, I could see his jaw working. Sometimes when he came home from work he took little blue books out of his briefcase. He made what he called a guide and let me help correct them. His students didn't have to know he exploited infant labor or that his TA was only five years old. It was fun and made me feel important. He told me about languages, and eventually it gave me the idea that if people could somehow map the movements of related languages, they would figure out the path of human migrations long before people thought of writing anything down. Somewhere in there, language and landscape and the story of how people got to where they were got all mixed up together.

My father and I come home from a long trudge in Riverside Park. We straggle single file through the lobby to reach the elevator, surprised to find it's already occupied by a slight, aging man, gray complected, in a gray overcoat and gray fedora, with a young man at his side.

The door slides shut, the cabin begins to rise. The slight gray man turns to my father, "Emilio, don't you recognize me?"

My father seems to notice him for the first time. "No," he says, "I'm afraid not."

"I am your brother, Abel," the gray man says.

We can hear the motor humming. The cabin hiccoughs to a stop. The door opens. My father gets out first.

I can see his jaw working. "Won't you come in?" he says to the man who is his brother. His voice betrays nothing. Nothing of what he must feel. If he feels...

He unlocks the door and stands aside to let the slight gray man, and the young man accompanying him, pass.

"This is Rosendo, your nephew," the gray man says to my father.

"Won't you sit down," my father says.

My father has a brother. I have an uncle, I have a cousin named Rosendo, same as my father's middle name. I have a family I didn't know I had and I can't understand what they're saying.

I am nine years old.

2. Screen Doors

After my Uncle Abel's surprise visit, nothing much changed. If my father spoke of him at all, it was to disparage his marriage to an Indian woman. "So if your name is Pineda y Galvan because your mother's name was Galvan, my name ought to be Pineda y Schweitzer, *then what was your father's name? Pineda y que?*" but no matter how much I persisted, he always turned silent.

Where was my grandmother, I wanted to know. What happened to her? How come he never talked about her? Any stories my father shared with me only chronicled a distant past, from before the Mexican Revolution of 1910, which forced him to flee Mexico along with my grandfather and his two older brothers, crossing the border at Brownsville, all four of them under assumed names.

Except when I asked questions, my parents hardly left me alone. My mother found me a doll, which she named Marie Louise. My father chose my French-speaking playmates. Subject to constant correction and punishment, anxiety consumed me. I must have begun to shut down early, but when I turned five, my mother rediscovered "summering," an expression current in her younger days, when she served as a Swiss governess to America's first families. She rented a summer sublet in Edgemere, a Long Island resort that must have seen better days. I don't remember the owner, a Mrs. Kubaya. She may have been an absent landlady, or maybe she just lived upstairs.

Our New York apartment, where I could never go out by myself, was the only world I knew, but in Edgemere all I had to do was push open the screen door. It whined and shuddered when I swung it wide; I fanned it open and shut over and over just to hear its thrum. It gave on Mrs. Kubaya's backyard, where the burned-out grasses grew neck high, but not so high they could camouflage the old rusting jalopy that lay outside the tumbling-down garage. Butterflies came to visit the tall weeds, white cabbage moths, yellow tiger-striped swallowtails and my favorites, the bright orange monarchs with black patterns on their wings. Sometimes, if they furled them long enough, they let me catch them. I discovered how furry their tiny bodies were and how their wings left a powdery dust on my fingers whenever I let them go. If I kept still long enough, a calico tabby showed up. I named him Tootsie Roll. When I pet him, he purred. Pet. Purr. Pet. Purr. I was learning predictability.

I learned about the days because my mother waited for the weekends when he came from the city to tell my father how I had "behaved." She said when children misbehaved they had to be sent away to the Vinegar School to get straightened out. Nights when I squirmed in bed unable to sleep, I kept picturing squat windowless buildings behind a cyclone fence. "Sit up straight, " my mother said. "Eat with your mouth closed." But at day's end, I would close my eyes and watch the lights under my eyelids shifting green and blue until I drifted off to sleep.

Flowers taught me the hours, the yellow and deep cherry red four o'clocks lining the road we followed weekends when my father came from the city and took me to the beach. Once he even took me out at night. A brightly lit row of attractions lined the boardwalk, offering dart games and prizes. I kept asking him for one of the pink celluloid Kewpie dolls, one with blue eyes and blonde hair. But before we headed back, he bought me a Mickey Mouse balloon instead. The man in the booth used a compressed air machine to blow it up. I watched the ears, the nose, the arms swell up. Just when it seemed ready to burst, the man snapped it off the machine. The rubber squealed as he tied the end into a knot. He stuck the knot between some cardboard feet to make the Mickey Mouse stand up. We took it back to Mrs. Kubaya's house.

Then there wasn't enough money to return to Edgemere anymore. Next summer my parents sent me away in the care of a Mrs. Harper, who kept a kindergarten. My father took me on the Long Island Railroad to Bay Shore, where we rode the ferry to Fire Island Pines. As I watched the dark waters of the bay slap against the pilings, I got scared he might be taking me to the school where children got straightened out. But I saw Mrs. Harper standing on the pier. A crowd of people waited for the boat to dock. Mrs. Harper put my things in a fire-engine-red racer wagon, which she pulled along the raised wooden walkways till we got to a house with an upstairs porch and a player piano inside.

I was in a world of other children. My homesickness vanished. Mornings, when Mrs. Harper was awake, we cut open the ends of shoe boxes to make peep shows with mermaids and starfish and sea lions inside, and we glued vermicelli-thin strips of blue and green cellophane to their lids, pretending it was the ocean. Sometimes when the weather got cloudy she let me put rolls in the player piano and pretend I could play, but on those sunny afternoons while Mrs. Harper napped we got to play doctor, feverishly mapping out our danger zones and exploring them more intently the long hours she left us by ourselves to play upstairs.

But best of all there was the gritty feel of sand on my bare feet, the heated smells of pine resin all along the wooden planks of the walkway leading to the beach, and the afternoons Mrs. Harper left me free to roam to collect shells and stones cast up by the tides until they got so heavy I couldn't carry them. To bend over horseshoe crabs in astonishment—never before had I seen such improbable creatures. And to watch the waves gathering themselves up into translucent spools of aquamarine before they hurled themselves on shore. As they washed back out to sea I could listen to the foam chattering and the mewling of sea birds as they swept past. I could skip or run for miles at the water's edge, free to sing above the water's roar, with no one to hear me, no one to stop me or pull me away, nothing to make me go home. There was no one to tell me what I was seeing or smelling or hearing or finding, no one to threaten or hit or pull me by the hair or force me to apologize.

But I wouldn't return to stay with Mrs. Harper again. Instead, my parents shipped me off to the New Jersey Pine Barrens. Giffy, a devout Quaker spinster, believed children should imbibe Shakespeare along with our tablespoon of malt. She lived in a house that smelled of another century. Sometimes hapless bats got trapped in the window curtains during the night. In contrast to the unbridled excess of Fire Island, those summers in American-small-town New Jersey seem more buttoned up, perhaps because we were just three little girls. In the lazy summer mornings we could explore the neighborhood, trailed by Shadow, the black dog who adopted us. In the afternoons we swam in the creek, where one day we found a beached catfish, its gills pumping frantically for air.

Giffy's vegetable garden yielded cosmos in all colors and okra and lima beans and tomatoes so voluptuous, it was nearly impossible not to sink my teeth into them before reaching the kitchen steps. At night, we played at Peaseblossom and Mustardseed under kerosene light, stumbling over the words of *A Midsummer Night's Dream*. And when it thundered, Giffy let us put on our bathing suits—a sure guarantee against lightning strike—and skylark through the showers. After the rains, fat toads hid under the dripping leaves of the hostas, and a spider—tiger striped, and big as a chicken's egg—made its home in the hydrangeas next door. Summer nights, I sat on the porch swing watching fireflies, which my pet praying mantises couldn't catch, caged as they were inside the screens where I'd left them nibbling on the fat corn worms I fed them.

Sometimes, when Giffy took off on her bike to buy more corn from the local farmer, we cut short our afternoon naps to make mischief, but on those rare afternoons when, as a special favor, she let me nap in her feather bed, the lure was just too great. I lay there nestled inside the mounds half-smothering me, listening to the trees in concert with the wind and watching the play of curtains swaying in the light.

Once we even got to visit the Atlantic City Boardwalk and see the circus. On the ride back, Hannah, Giffy's friend, stopped her 1934 Studebaker just short of crushing a turtle limping across the road—which was how Cleopatra ambled into my life, with her yellow markings and her right front foot shorn of toes—the result of some accident or other misadventure. Next spring, she laid a clutch of tiny eggs, giving life to five tiny yellow-striped turtles emerging from their shells. One time I even came upon hundreds of her relatives—a turtle migration—lumbering over the grasses, making for the creek.

But Fire Island stayed with me: the brush of salt air, the smell of sand baking in the noonday sun, the never-ending pound of surf, and above all the taste of freedom. And if sex was no longer present in those furtive afternoons while our minder napped, its imprint could become the stuff of art. Until Hannah, come for a visit, spied me crouched outside the kitchen where she sat and asked to see what I was drawing.

At summer's end, when Giffy put me on the train back home to the city, I had no way of knowing I'd never be back, but as fall set in a package came from her. Inside was a scattering of precious monarch butterflies, dead from the first frost. It was her way of saying goodbye. There would be no more summers away from my parents' watchful eyes or free of their punishing hands. Soon I lapsed into some kind of twilight. My mind wandered in school. Nothing could rekindle the memory of Giffy's chicken with dumplings on Sundays or her lima beans in cream sauce. I stopped eating. I began to worry that if I ever found myself in jail for life, I would have to take enough with me of what I remembered never to feel bored.

Day Two

As news of detainee abuse began to make headlines, Jean Blum began keeping files of their letters and their complaints, as well as background materials, official "incident" reports, complaint forms filed with the Passaic County Jail administration, and detainees' letters to her and others, some attesting to conditions still unimagined and unknown to most Americans. The incidents outlined here only begin to describe the kind of conditions the detainees were enduring then and that more than four hundred thousand of them, many of them unaccompanied children, are forced to endure still now.

Blum's first report, running to four pages, documents the statements of four Asian detainees. The guards ordered the prisoners to face the bars, aiming chemical spray inches from their faces. They grabbed one prisoner by the arm and the neck, slapping and pushing him down the hall where the video cameras couldn't film. They threw him to the ground, where they continued to punch him before handcuffing him and taking him to the medical unit. Later they threw him into the hole.... For four days in solitary he requested meds and to see a doctor, to no avail. On the fifth day, two officers took him to a hearing, telling him he was charged with attempt to assault. Eventually he was found innocent and the case was dismissed.

A February 28, 2006, statement from newly arrived detainee Luis del Orbe states:

> [When I arrived at] the Passaic County Jail... I was held in two separate holding cells at different [times] until I was issued a sleeping mat and placed in a dormitory at 9:35 pm.... At all times these cells are at nearly [three] times over their maximum capacity.... I was escorted to a basement dormitory.... This dormitory has forty-eight sleeping bunks, yet eighty-nine individuals are expected to sleep there. Through the four days and three nights I was there, the number of individuals increased as more of the recently arrested [were] brought in. Those who are unable to sleep in a bed are given plastic mat containers, which are placed at any available space on the floor. Those who did not get these plastic mat containers must place their mats in any available floor space...; anyone needing to use the toilet facilities must... hurtle over those individuals sleeping on the floor....
>
> One of the individuals going through his drug... withdrawals vomited on me. Since there was no hot water available, I had to take a cold shower and be given new jail clothing.... Due to the poor ventilation... there was at all [times] a temperature above 90 degrees.... Conditions... were not made any better when the K-9 unit being handled by Corporal Mercado defecated on the floor of the dormitory, a space [it] just so [happened] is at face level where I was sleeping on the floor.

It came to me that my father was flawed. We had been invited to spend the day in New Jersey with my parents' friends. It was hot. After lunch everyone straggled out onto the porch. I listened while the grownups talked. Pretty soon my father began talking about Masons and Jews. As he grew increasingly agitated, his voice rose. I could see discomfort playing on the faces of the company. I couldn't quite grasp what my father said, but beneath I sensed the fear, the paranoid tilt toward violence. My tears came. No one thought to notice the small girl sitting in the corner crying.

"Why did you marry my mother?" I was about ten years old the first time I asked. My father pretended not to hear, I could see his jaw working, but when I kept asking, he answered at last. There were some things I wouldn't be able to understand. Just what they were he couldn't explain, not until I "got older." He never thought to say exactly how old I might have to be.

Winter set in. One day we went walking along a deserted stretch of Riverside Drive. The winds had stripped the tree limbs bare. One leaf still clung to a lower branch. When I pointed to it, he told me I was mistaken. It was a chrysalis. Inside, a caterpillar had knit its winter coat. Come spring, when the weather warmed, it would hatch. A butterfly would step out newborn into the world. He said if I wanted to, we could take it home, where we could put it out all winter outside my bedroom window and wait for it to hatch. He helped me stand on his shoulders, holding me fast just long enough to reach the twig where the caterpillar had spun its home. I snapped it off.

We found an empty cake box to put it in. Through the long winter's snows, it lay outside, held safe inside the window guard. Sometimes the box lay buried in snow, but by the time the snow began to melt, seeing it out there had become so familiar, I had forgotten all about it.

Lent came. I wasn't feeling well. My head throbbed so badly my mother kept me home from school. And then I nearly died. My mother sat by my bedside, sponging my forehead, ringing the wash cloth out in the enamel basin on the bedside table. Over and over I could hear the water dripping in the basin. The bed kept making whooshing sounds, rising higher and higher, lifting me up feet first, then sweeping me down, down deep, and out, like a wave that left me floating somewhere inside the darkness. There were stars of light inside it, as though someone had poked pinpricks in the night.

I couldn't lift my head to drink. My father got a baby bottle so I could drink lying down. Sometimes above the buzzing in my ears I could hear my parents in the corridor outside. I couldn't make out what they were whispering, but I knew. They were talking with the pediatrician our family doctor sent for when he realized my deadly case of measles put him way beyond his depth.

A day after the new doctor gave me a shot, the buzzing stopped, and the bed lay flat once more. I was a month recovering. I had forgotten what my legs felt like. My mother had to hook her arm under my knees to get me out of bed.

It was Easter. Outside in the street, peddlers were selling flowers from their horse-drawn carts. Although my bedroom window gave on the courtyard, I could hear them calling in the street. "Lilies, violets, roses..." My mother left my bedside just long enough to buy me a hyacinth. It was pink, like the dresses she made me wear. She put it on the sill where I could see it by the open window.

When I was strong enough to get up, the cake box still lay outside. Out of curiosity I raised the lid. Inside the box was gray. What was that extra piece of crumpled cardboard doing there? Something moved, a slight movement, maybe because my hand disturbed the box. I held still. It moved again. One of its folds opened with a slight pop. An eye appeared, dark as a no-moon night. An hour later, inside the winter cake box was a lavender-colored moth fully formed. Its feathery feelers trembled in an absent wind. And as I watched, its furry body began pumping out hundreds of eggs, none of them bigger than an amaranth seed.

I ran to tell my father. He stayed quiet for some time before getting up from his chair. He searched for a book on one of his bedroom shelves. He leafed through it till he found what he was looking for. He stroked the page flat with his hand before he began to read.

The words were Spanish, words I couldn't understand. But it wasn't his voice anymore. It came from some other place inside. When he was finished he closed the book.

"Why are you crying?" I asked him.

"Because it's very beautiful," he said.

But that may not be quite the truth. Although they occurred separately, here I have placed these two events together because that is how I want to remember him: The one to cherish me as an infant, the one who took me out, the one who read to me and told me stories. The one who recognized in almost every occasion something to be wondered at. It was on his shoulders I stood that time in the heart of winter, snapping a branch off a sycamore. Someone for whom taking a chrysalis home was not unthinkable, someone who once read a poem to me in a language I couldn't understand.

Something haunted my father. I had no way of knowing what it was. In the early years, I must have played out his anxiety. But no one gave it a name because no one knew how to speak it. Not my teachers, if they ever knew its source, not my mentors, if they even knew what caused it. And certainly not my parents, not my mother, either because she never knew or if she did, she never said because she liked keeping things to herself and preferred never to share anything with me.

And my father? I have to think that in some misguided way, he thought it best to keep his terror to himself.

What is inescapable is that, no matter how impenetrable the silence, children are never impervious (because we are all animals and contain the memory of that world within us, the preverbal world of other creatures). They sense any turbulence. And although they experience *home* in the things that surround them, the membrane of that cocoon in its fundamental smells, the wonder of its colors, its textures (and the memory of fur), that in no way insulates them from more elemental things. And that is why I swam in a miasma of mute fear throughout my childhood, a fear that, if I ever gave it a name, was that one day, with no warning, my parents *might* disappear.

Might. The name of fear itself.

3. Freedom

From the age of seven I knew theater had to be where I belonged, a place where I could be someone else. When I was barely six, despite the protestations of my playmates and although I was the smallest, I claimed the giant's role in an improvised play of "Jack and the Beanstalk." In high school, by the time we put on our senior play, I was bit. Assigned a meager sixteen lines in the Spanish-inflected accent of a Latina, the role came with a foxy turn-of-the-century veiled hat that cocked rakishly over one eye, a tight bodice with leg o' mutton sleeves, and a full bustle skirt in ravishing shades of deep cherry red, all supplied to my measurements by a professional stage supply house. So outfitted, I swept onstage to deliver my sixteen lines with undisguised aplomb. It was decidedly not a good thing that my parents were present to witness the display. Repressed as they were, nonetheless they recognized the cherry-red flag of budding eroticism—or budding whatever it was.

When it came time to choose a college, convinced that an English major would guarantee what my father called "your social security for life," he insisted I attend a serious institution and not the drama school of my choice. A full scholarship to Barnard College sealed my fate. But I was curious. How was it that, in his youth, newly immigrated to the United States, he had been able to attend Harvard? Had he applied for a scholarship too? "Oh, no," he dismissed the idea, "not for people of our class." Then how had he managed? "Oh," he shrugged, "people owed my father favors."

My parents were all too aware that, serious or not, Barnard wasn't going to offer any of my convent high school's tepid little tea dances, and although rock 'n' roll had not yet made the cultural scene, sex most certainly had. Early in my freshman year I auditioned for Columbia Players and over stiff competition won a coveted role in T. S. Eliot's *Murder in the Cathedral*. My parents' reaction to my grab at freedom wasn't long in coming. Rules were rules: nine o'clock curfew, no unsupervised dating, and absolutely no theatrical touring, not to Washington, D.C., or Lancaster, Pennsylvania, or Baltimore, Maryland, and certainly not in mixed company. The answer was an implacable *no*. I saw what promised to be a brilliant career go up in flames.

I chose a Saturday morning to stage a performance calculated to bring them to heel. My theatrics went so far overboard, it had them flummoxed, quite stumped about what to do. I suggested they call my godmother, who promptly stepped out from the wings, but as she took in my tirade, I saw the look of concern darkening her face. In one of my parents' unguarded moments, I managed a whispered aside: "It's just a performance."

It may have been the summit of my career because the following weekend I boarded the tour bus with the cast of twenty Columbia Players and our crew, raucously singing union songs in three-part harmony all the way to D.C., and I forged an alliance with my godmother that would last her lifetime. No longer was she Jeanne, or "petite Jeanne" as my father diminutively preferred, but Mayenne, my own childhood name for her.

Much later she shared the story of the time she agreed to babysit me at her apartment. "I'm going home," I announced. "Go ahead," she challenged me right back, "goodbye." Probably that *goodbye* was a genuine expression of her feeling for me at the time. Deep down, she confessed she never did much care for little kids, not until they reached their adolescence. Even so, in those early years, she never missed a birthday. Some of the most exquisite books of my childhood—an illustrated *Wind in the Willows*, collected stories of Oscar Wilde—came from her, always carefully wrapped, accompanied by a card in her unmistakable handwriting, the echo of each word stretched out in a protracted line long after it ended.

Every summer when she returned to France, she left me her apartment key and a small reward for feeding her cat and tidying his litter box. After I'd done my chores, I could stay over the long summer afternoons. It was on her shelves I first discovered Jean Genet, Nathalie Sarraute, Eugène Ionesco, and, best of all, Sam Beckett.

She must have been aware that even early on, the theater was my passion. On my twelfth birthday, after treating me to a Rabelaisian meal (I ordered a Chateaubriand and choked down every last morsel) she invited me to a matinee of *Henry V*, where from the moment Leslie Banks bowed and swept his plumed hat off to speak the prologue, I forgot everything: My godmother, the row of plush seats where we sat, the Chateaubriand turning to lead in the pit of my stomach. I *became* the sweeping hat, the fat pearl earring dangling from his ear, the smartly turned leg, the buckle shoes. The words and all the hyperbolic gestures set me on fire.

I could do that!

There was no doubt that for me, it was the theater that I loved, but aside from only two drama courses on offer, Barnard held little appeal. Unengaged by Matthew Arnold and the English curriculum, I continued reading outside the list: Merton, Andreyev, Isaac Babel, and Borowski.

"The Barnard woman combines marriage with a career" was the dean's mantra at the time. The word *career* with its implied attaché case and dress-for-success suit repelled me. If nothing else, for someone theatrically inclined as I was, its parade of goofy professors offered subjects ripe for poking fun, in particular the president herself, who described her wedding night as so hygienically thrilling, she had no idea just exactly what it was her husband was up to—this in front of the vividly Technicolor four-by-six-foot chart of the female pudendum displayed on the hygiene class blackboard just behind the podium where she lectured.

A year, Mondays through Fridays, of early morning Spanish class gave me recurring nightmares in which either I turned up late, still wearing my pajamas, or failed to show at all—until one morning, barely awake, I surprised my father, who was tiptoeing into my room, turning off the alarm. We could speak French at home as much as we liked, but he had no intention of my ever learning Spanish.

Midway through my sophomore year, my college grades were tanking. Without my scholarship, I'd have to return to the daily grind I'd already sampled during those summers I took survival jobs on Wall Street or in the Garment District. At the eleventh hour, my advisor, who as a French teacher happened to have trained sometime back under my godmother's mentorship, thought to contact her.

Mayenne summoned me. I knew I'd have to admit to a shame I had managed to keep from her—the violence at home, my father's beatings. She expressed disbelief at first—this after divorcing an American soldier husband who hit her regularly. But perhaps her scars were not so deeply buried she couldn't take me at my word. A visit to my parents was in order. She convinced them to lighten up and leave their daughter room enough to breathe.

With my newfound freedom, I stayed away from home as much as possible. I made a stab at sweet-talking a boyfriend who shied away with all the prudery he'd inherited from his six-foot-tall, lantern-jawed mother, but not so quickly he couldn't suggest that the person I *really* needed to meet was his aging Jewish piano teacher from Saint Petersburg. An orotund, balding little man, with three hairs combed over an otherwise bare scalp, his flag of defiance against the decline of old age, Sascha Hoffman came from a family of rich Jewish merchants who first prospered in Czarist Russia.

He took an immediate shine to me. *Tetard*, he liked to call me, French for *tadpole*, "because she has beeg head but no body." He used his name for me at every opportunity: "Tetard, apparat, s'il te plait." The *apparat* was his inhaler, which he applied whenever paroxysmal coughing threatened to choke him. If he took note of my father at all, it was to call him "un petit señorito avec des bigotes bien tournées" (a stuck-up little snob with twirled-up mustaches).

Once a month on Fridays he held a gathering. His servant, Ivanovna, would slope along the scuffed-up corridor in her foot wrappings opening to my ring. He would send me out to buy herring in sour cream (I was not yet of age to resupply the vodka) while Ivanovna sliced onions and dark bread, and the festivities got under way, four ingredients and an equal number of disreputable Russian expatriate friends—all musicians—he'd inherited from his Paris nightclub days before the war. He'd introduce me proudly. "Thees ees Tetard, mais elle a quelque chose dans le ventre," and he would explain about my head and my stunted anatomy, for which I was supposed to compensate with smarts. He was the first adult in my life to suggest I might add up to something after all, maybe even something *raisonable*.

Weekly visits became a habit. He was usually giving lessons, unless of course he sat alone at the keyboard. Once Ivanovna let me in, I'd tiptoe down the long corridor so as not to startle him. He'd stop playing and pat the piano bench for me to sit. And slowly I took in the stories. They started modestly: as a young man, in North Africa, how he'd concertized with Rubinstein, *un drôle de canard*—a strange bird. He was writing something, a book of short stories. How life in Paris as a café musician got on his nerves, how slowly he found himself succumbing to ennui. How he sat on the terrace of a neighborhood bistro, waiting in vain for a woman who never showed up, a woman he referred to as *ma femme verte*, his green woman. I never discovered whether she reminded him of *Madame Matisse*, the Impressionist canvas painted predominantly in shades of verdigris, or if she suffered from a permanent state of nausea. That was *avant-guerre*, before the Germans caught up with him and hauled him off to a concentration camp. Not a problem really—he escaped. Three times! But it did his tuberculosis no good. He turned to me solemnly: "The people who survived were the rich ones who, even when they were freezing, had the memory of their fur coats to keep them warm. But remember," he waved an admonishing finger, "only those survive whose spirits are intact."

His coughing was getting worse, and, even though he kept giving lessons, he didn't quite know how he was going to pay Ivanovna; he had to buy gasoline for Samson, his derelict jalopy, "because Samson ees strrrrong, and notheeng can stop heem"; he was having trouble buying new cartridges for his inhaler. I'd made what I thought of as a killing at my last summer job as a Wall Street cable clerk, trading dollars for pounds sterling, with Société Générale banking on the spread. It seemed quite natural to buy his cartridges for him. And all the while, coughing, almost choking, he continued teaching a parade of students, a different one every hour.

Barely a month later the phone rang. It was Walter, my bashful boyfriend's older brother. I sensed what he would tell me. After a night of drinking vodka and losing at poker, Sascha left at dawn, driving Samson home. He'd gone to bed and never awakened. His old jalopy had outlived him.

I remember the upscale Lexington Avenue funeral parlor paid for by his bother Victor, who suddenly appeared out of nowhere, and how I dropped my mother's precious Swiss edelweiss, the everlasting flower, into the casket just before they sealed it shut, before Walter told me the story Sascha surely never wanted me to hear: how, when he contracted tuberculosis as a young man, his wealthy family could afford to send him to a sanatorium near Geneva, where he met Lenin, later accompanying him to the Finland Station, and how, like Isaac Babel, who wanted to prove Jews are not cowards, he joined an execution squad. Until one fine day he was moved to ditch his rifle and leave the killing ground behind, the day a sailor appeared in the lineup, a red-headed giant who stared him down and challenged him to shoot.

Sometime in my sophomore year, alerted that a group of French students were rehearsing in the college theater, I dropped by to have a look. The company was staging Molière to baroque musical accompaniment. I stopped long enough to listen. Someone was tootling expertly on the recorder. Eventually, we got to talking. He was French, born in Paris. At the time, he was reading Camus' *La Peste*. His name was Felix, middle name Theophile, a name he preferred never to use.

Although any search for a partner was the very last thing on my mind at the time, I took a fancy to him at once. I sensed this must not be an ordinary encounter. I came up with a ploy. If he needed to make the old theater upright sound like a harpsichord, I told him how to prepare it. I convinced him to go off with me to the local hardware to buy the necessary thumbtacks, not necessarily the romantic encounter I might have fantasized, but it would do as second best. Alas! as we came to the first street corner, he parted ways. His purveyor of tacks was not my purveyor of tacks. But the following fall, cast in a student-authored play (by Marion Magid, my classmate, later editor of *Commentary*) I caught sight of him outside my dressing room. He had returned to find me.

I believed that in some mysterious way, Sascha had sent him to me. To my great relief—especially given my social awkwardness—ours was not the classic American romance. There was no Noah's-Ark two-by-two dating, none of the posturing, none of the competition, none of the "waiting for the phone to ring." From the start, language drew us together in a cozy kind of intimacy. It tapped a whole cultural complex as well, one in which I had already found meaning.

We spent our time in the company of La Bande, a bunch of French-speaking students. Pure élan carried us. We were together as a group, and we understood that we would enjoy our private moments too. Felix listened to my stories with such empathy, it calmed the chronic anxiety I didn't even know I felt. That first winter we spent long hours in a local pizzeria whose indulgent owner allowed us to stay warm long after we'd wolfed down the last slice. But if I could remember moment to moment the details of my childhood, Felix drew blanks for most of his, much of it spent in hiding in occupied France. At the age of three his single mother felt compelled to farm him out to a childless couple living in Normandy who raised him as their own. Later, when he developed tuberculosis, she transferred him to what was then called a preventorium. There he learned that he was Jewish from other children's taunts, and that he was directly and personally responsible for killing *l'enfant Jésus*.

His early guardians never forgot him. As the war broke out, and train loads of Jewish children began to be transported to the death camps, the freight trains passed through their Normandy village. Daily they made their way to the station, hoping to spot him and pull him from the train. In 1940, when Germany invaded, his mother sent him, along with his best friend, to La Bourboule, a small town in the "free zone," seventy kilometers north of Nazi headquarters in Clermont-Ferrand. As the German army rolled into Paris one month later, his mother joined him. He was nine years old. It was the first time in six years he had lived with her. In La Bourboule, he had his first experience of a father—actually a stepfather—who raised him as his own. At war's end in 1945, when he returned with his mother to Paris, they found their apartment ransacked. "Oh," explained their neighbors, "we thought you wouldn't be coming back."

As Eastern Europe disgorged the bones of prisoners living and dead, an emaciated Emmanuel Levinas made his way from a German work camp where he had been held as a prisoner of war, to a Jewish lycée outside of Paris, which hired him. A philosopher of considerable standing already then, he became Felix's mentor. By the time of his death in 1995, Levinas had become recognized as France's greatest ethicist. It was these same ethical qualities that drew Felix to me: his compassion, his sense, deeply ingrained, of justice, a concept quintessentially Jewish, in which the practice of charity is considered justice due, and later, when he set up medical practice, the generosity and good nature with which he related to all his patients.

When after the war his mother accepted the charge of ORT, a Jewish organization, to establish a home for some of the thousands of children of deportees, Felix gave voice to his feelings about having been farmed out during so many of his childhood years. But when he questioned why she'd taken on the burden of so many others when she seemed to have so little time for him, she temporized. After all, her charges were that much more entitled because they had no parents left at all.

That certain sense of absence held us together in those early years. It was the absence of something that ought to have been ours but that remained unspoken, and that somehow had been denied. Much later I began to think it had been this need of his, still unresolved, which—without even being entirely conscious of it—called to me because I had not yet articulated my own need, that by nurturing someone I deeply loved I could somehow create a quality of home that my own childhood had sorely lacked.

If I felt somehow Felix had been Sascha's gift to me, in turn Felix made me the gift of Henry. "If you want to know what genius looks like," was how he introduced me to his polymath Columbia classmate. By then, emancipated at last, I was renting a third-floor walkup near Columbia for sixty-five dollars a month. It was furnished in Salvation Army splendor: a couch, dining set, and derelict upright piano made up the living room. The bedroom, pink as monkey puke, was so narrow, you had to fall into bed once you entered it. But the landlady was benevolent and the stairs good exercise.

Once a week, Henry climbed my three flights to pay me a visit. No matter how down at the heel, he arrived with a rumpled bag of tangerines and a briefcase bulging to the limit with books on the subject he happened to have taken up at the moment—quantum mechanics was the first in the series. With a sallow complexion and teeth ridged with a deposit of what appeared to be green algae, he was so slight of build, when I hugged him too suddenly, I discovered I could lift him high enough to sweep him off the ground. He preferred not to change his shirt until the inner collar turned dim. I never quite discovered when the warning light appeared, but it was his signal to find a menswear store and exchange it for a new one. He applied the same principles to shoes and socks. But that especially chill winter, he lacked an overcoat, a need I quickly filled through an intervention with a onetime beau and scion of a menswear manufacturer.

Henry's English still bore traces of Polish; the cast of his features, especially his ski-jump nose, suggested Polish origins, but his ethnicity had cost him dearly. Like Felix and like Sascha before him, Henry was Jewish. Early in our friendship, when pneumonia kept me in bed for a month, he paid me one of his weekly visits, briefcase and tangerines in tow. Still bundled in his newly acquired winter coat, he sat at the edge of my sickbed. I remember that visit to this day. Years later, fearing I had lost contact with him permanently, I wrote "Touching Henry," a short story published in *580 Split*, imagining that, if by some miracle chance he were to read it, he might be prompted to get in touch with me. I hear his voice speaking to me still:

> In the ghetto, kids kept going through the sewers into Warsaw, and sometimes they would come back bringing food. But

sometimes they wouldn't come back and we didn't know what happened to them. The old people began to die. You would see them, rolled over in the gutter. And little children. Everyone was hungry all the time. And the ghetto leaders tried negotiating, but nothing changed. And then it was the Uprising. For nearly three months, maybe longer, and the kids leading it were only eighteen! Eighteen! Imagine! When the fighting started they made us go down in the bunkers, my mother, my father, and me.

We had to be very quiet in the bunker because they could hear everything underneath the ground, the Germans with their big ears, they could even hear rats scurrying. We had to be very still, talk only in whispers especially at night. There was a pregnant woman in the bunker with us. And one night she gave birth, and she had no milk to feed the child, and it wailed and wailed, and she tried to stop its mouth with her hand. And the men decided it had to be killed because the big ears would pick up its cries of hunger, and so they smothered it, and the wailing stopped.

And all the while you sit at the edge of my bed, and you aren't crying. No sound escapes you, but the wet leaps from your eyes, courses down your cheeks in rivulets; hangs momentarily from your chin before splashing onto your coat, and you make no effort to wipe it away. You go on whispering in your bunker voice.

And so they killed it. They had to because of the big ears. And then they found us. They raised the hatch.

—EVERYONE OUT WITH THEIR HANDS UP. YOU HAVE THREE MINUTES. THREE MINUTES AND THEN WE BLOW THE BUNKER UP.

And you laugh that hair-raising laugh of yours.

We came up with our hands on our heads, my mother, my father, and me. But not everyone came out. Some stayed. And after they herded us down the street, and out of the ghetto, we heard the explosions. And we knew they were dead, the ones who stayed behind.

And they marched us to the railroad yard. This time there was no out. They separated us. The women to the left. The men to the right. I never saw my mother again.

When we marched across the countryside in the freezing cold, we had to sleep in ditches. One night when my father thought I was asleep, I heard him say to the man lying next to him, "that's my son, sleeping there. I wish he would be dead."

Your tears stream down. You make no sound, no sob, no cry, not even a whimper. Then you see I'm crying. . . . And when I touch your hands, I discover they're wet. And I say, "Henry, somewhere there must be a god who hears, who grieves."

But that particular visit was far from typical. Most of the time we spent the time clowning. His laugh was more of a horse's neigh. No one else could make me howl quite so uncontrollably. Between visits, there were midnight phone calls from the switchboard he operated as a night clerk. He had dropped in on Theodor Gaster to exchange thoughts about the Gospel of Thomas, or Margaret Mead had invited him to view a film of her giving birth. And the time he struck up a conversation with Norbert Wiener on the subject of cybernetics, or the time he met with Roman Jakobson at Harvard to mull over some obscure aspect of linguistics. Or he paid a visit to Meyer Schapiro to discuss scholarly speculation as to why da Vinci might have persisted for twenty years refining the *Mona Lisa*. No matter how run down at the heel, no matter the state of his shirt collars, he was educating himself, seeking people out, taking for granted that they would engage with him, not just as their interlocutor but as a peer. He never became affiliated with an institution of higher learning, although much later, Felix and I would wire him money so he could attend lectures at the Sorbonne and—as he wrote—sit at the feet of Simone de Beauvoir and Jean-Paul Sartre.

Nowadays, we give lip service to role models. Such people—whoever they are—sound flat and lacking much topography. If Sascha managed to convince me that somehow I might amount to something, Henry was giving me some insight as to how I might attempt it—whatever it was. He was an original, with his horse's laugh and his dim collars, which only added dimension to the mix. In the meantime, we had more clowning to do, more outrageous humor to trade.

More midnight telephone calls to catch up on his intellectual—and amorous—pursuits.

After our loan to him, Felix and I lost track of him. On my frequent visits to New York, where I kept appointments with my then-literary agent and paid visits to my son, I searched for him on the Upper West Side in all his old stomping grounds. I peered in the windows of fast-moving subway cars, straining for a glimpse of him. And then, one year summering in New York, on a steaming evening I took a stroll down Broadway. Standing on the southwest corner of Eighty-Sixth Street stood a little old man with a tiny ski-jump nose. Surprised by joy, I blurted his name. My whoop must have sounded more like an accusation, but, dizzy with happiness, I thought nothing of sweeping him off the ground! "Where have you been? Where did you disappear to all these years!" I am sure he found my reaction intimidating. He hedged for a time, promising to be in touch the following week, but the very next day the phone call came. "Don't you think I'm a failure, I was always going to be this intellectual big shot," he kept repeating. At last I stopped him. "I'm not going to indulge you, Henry. I'm not a failure. And if I'm not a failure, it's because of you, because of the example you set me."

In the silence I could hear him breathing.

We met on Riverside Drive. We caught up with all the intervening years. At last, he eyed my quizzically. "Do you know why I disappeared?" I shook my head. "I was never able to repay you." I could see his distress. "Forget it. That was so long ago. I'm so happy to have found you!" But the sounds of traffic suddenly disappeared, and the children playing in the sand pile, the wind in the elm trees. Our conversation turned dark because he was saying, "I came to see you every week because I told myself, if I could just wait till the next visit, I would have survived another week. Because you had something there to hold me if I could only just wait the other six days out."

Felix, Henry, and Sascha, these were my mentors. all of them were men, all of them Jewish; in varying degrees, their lives had been grotesquely bent off course by the twentieth century's great tragedy.

Above all, they knew who they were. I think what drew me to them was the kind of gravitas that comes from living on the edge. I wanted that kind of being for myself, even if I had to borrow it. In coming to love them, I made their history my own. That history marking the abyss of what human nature could become would become the root of my life's activism; it would deepen the scope of my art and inform my way of being in the world.

Day Three

Although detainees held in "administrative detention" are not classified as criminals, their treatment is comparable to that of ordinary prisoners. For example, Joseph Elchin's June 2005 letter to Blum states that, despite the initiatives on his behalf by the public defender and the repeated pleas of his sister, who wished to notify him that his mother was dying and had been rushed to the hospital to be placed on a ventilator, he was not allowed to speak to her; "as a matter of fact, no one from this institution ever informed me of anything. I [only] learned of the situation when I called home."

The Passaic County Sheriff's department and the jail warden refused him the privilege of visiting his mother on her deathbed before she was removed from the ventilator which was keeping her alive. "Judge Guzman ... denied such [a] bedside visit, stating that 'if I wanted to pay my last respects I could do so at the funeral.'" But in fact, arrangements for Elchin to attend his mother's funeral were denied when, despite intercession by his sister and the public defender, Judge Guzman refused to sign the order.

The Elchin case, a criminal one, can be compared to one affecting an immigrant detainee. In a letter dated September 26, 2005, addressed to Judge Patricia E. Henry, Juliette Tucker, who was about to be deported to Jamaica, writes:

> I have been in the United States for eight years and have never had any criminal involvement. As you know I have three beautiful children who need their mother.... I am pleading not so much for myself, but for my children.... Please take this plea into consideration by allow-

ing me to take all three children with me to Jamaica.... My plan is to go to Jamaica first and shortly after I send for my children.... Due to this, your Honor, I will [sic] truly like to see my children before I leave on the 24 October, 2005. Therefore with all humbleness I am seeking your compassion by asking you please, your Honor, allow me a visit with my children. Please, your Honor, I don't want to abandon my children due to ... circumstances beyond my control. I am asking you please to grant me one favor to say goodbye and don't take my motherly rights away from me.

Although Blum tried to effect an intervention on her behalf, Juliette Tucker was ordered deported without being allowed to see her children.

Late in life, after 9/11 and Katrina's devastation, I first turned to nonfiction, publishing a feature-length article about deportation and immigrant detention pegged on Jean Blum and her work (see appendix), at once echoing my connection to the Holocaust of 1939–1945, and linking it to today's vast tide of migrations—the human Holocaust of more recent times. Without realizing it at first, I had begun the journey that would lead me to discover my true origins.

II

The Way to Art

II

The Way to Art

4. Divorcing Mom and Dad

As my graduating college class thrilled to the remarks of that year's keynote speaker, I trolled New York's old Factory District, along Spring and Green Streets for the part-time job that would free up enough time for me to hit Broadway with a puffed-up résumé. But the call of the theater was just too great. At the last minute, changing plans, I joined a summer stock company playing the Poconos, where I managed to wangle a waitering spot for Felix. In that setting, the caliber of what passed for theater may have been banal and without imagination, but the chance to be together and away from family prying outweighed the predictable offerings of any summer stock summer, no matter how third rate.

There was a price to pay, but I would not discover what it was until my return to New York at summer's end, when my parents met me at the door with an ultimatum: move out at once. That night. They had plans to rent my room and they wanted me out. Wherever I might find lodging that night or any future time was none of their concern.

Arianne, one of La Bande's members and my close college friend, offered to rent me a room, and that's where I wound up. My living with her and her husband, Marco, allowed theater rounds two afternoons a week and provided their chaotic household with babysitting services. I found the factory job at once, but acting assignments failed to materialize, and, given the relatively tame state of New York theater in the fifties, it was probably a good thing after all. In the meantime, rounds offered me a smorgasbord of sociological sleuthing, my passion by default, in the sleazy world of Broadway, with its smarmy, cigar-smoking agents and producers bent on feeding their egos and their couches with reservoirs of aspiring young starlets. Had I discovered the Living Theatre, which was getting its start performing in West End Avenue's living rooms at the time, I might have run away and joined the circus, but as it happened my father suffered a heart attack—his first—and working part time, my off hours allowed me to visit him in the hospital. He made a stunning recovery—enough to inconvenience my life and jeopardize the life of Arianne and her children in a way I could never have imagined.

When La Bande still got together from time to time, Marco, Arianne's husband, hinted he was making plans. What they were exactly, he fell short of making clear. Eventually he announced that he'd taken out an insurance policy. Six months to the day after it took effect, as he washed the windows of their top-floor flat, he plunged down seven stories to his death.

To our surprise, we learned Marco had been a veteran. (He may have suffered from post-traumatic stress disorder, a condition still unrecognized in the day.) He received a full dress funeral, complete with "Taps" and the U.S. flag, ceremonially folded in a fat triangle and placed in his devastated widow's hands. We all banded together to help her grieve; we found daycare for her two little girls, launched an expedition to Hester Street to buy two steamer trunks cavernous enough to fit all her belongings. At last we accompanied the little family to the West Side pier, where we waved disconsolately as they boarded ship for France.

Overwhelmed by the horror of it, I had heedlessly blurted my feelings at home. Soon thereafter, I learned my father had sent an anonymous letter to the insurance company advising them that Marco's death had not been accidental. When the company launched an investigation, I felt my own indiscretion was to blame. The economic future of Arianne and her two small girls hung in the balance. I am not exactly sure how the idea of forensic photography came to me, probably because a kindly neighbor living on a lower floor had showed us her windowpane: there they were, the unmistakable soapy hand prints of someone grasping at any last-minute salvation on the way down to his death. Inquiries yielded lower windowpanes with similar ghostly hand prints. I found a photographer before any of the evidence could be washed away.

Eventually, long after I moved again, severing all connection with my family, the insurance company settled. Not long afterward, I spied my father crossing Broadway in the far distance. Recognizing his bent figure, even at that distance, made me realize how old and weary he had become. It no longer made me sad. I simply accepted our estrangement as a fact of life.

La Bande broke up soon afterward. For me and Felix, real life had made its claim. Although I waited a year, the time I needed to prove to myself that I could provide my own support, we decided the time had come to marry. I would take my husband's name. At the time, if I pondered it at all, I considered that it would provide a welcome erasure of a troubled past. That I was putting the search for my true identity on ice never once occurred to me.

A photograph I took of Felix at that time shows a shock of auburn hair swept up above a high forehead, a strong sense of presence animating a generous smile (fig. 4), but introducing him to my parents proved to be a disaster. It improved matters even less when they discovered he was Jewish, and a socialist at that. But from the moment she first laid eyes on him, Felix was a hands-down hit with my godmother. She clapped her hands, squealing with delight, "oh, what magnificent teeth!" "Quelles magnifiques dents. Montre-moi tes dents!" Aside from his dentition, it was his love of Rabelais and especially of his earthiness that utterly won her heart. They sat together on her couch, guffawing over page after scurrilous page, altogether oblivious to me.

Given Felix's intern's salary of a hundred dollars a month, our last-minute visit to city hall's marriage bureau had much to recommend it: between his medical school finals, moving into our first flat, and leaving for our honeymoon, the date could be kept fairly fluid; as a low-profile arrangement, it ruled out the formal wedding reception

FIG. 4. "A photograph I took of [my husband] at that time." Felix Leneman.

and dinner and certain bankruptcy, and above all, it dispensed with a showing by the parents of the bride. Mayenne stood in for my family. The mise-en-scène included five guests, an American flag, next to it a cuspidor, and a city clerk whose Brooklynese pronounced us "jerned" as man and wife. We celebrated with a luncheon in a Little Italy watering hole favored by the Mafia and noted, along with the penne marinara, for its many gangland hits. Once the festivities drew to a close, we dropped into the IRT for a quick trip home. Out of sheer excitement I spiked a temperature of 103, but Felix cooled any thought of ardor with an appointment with his dentist. The honeymoon would have to wait until we left for Mexico.

Gringa.

Rosendo, my favorite Mexican cousin, eyes me affectionately.

It's the first time anyone's ever called me *gringa*. I smile back lightheartedly. We sit at an outdoor cantina sipping beer. Next to me sits my husband of barely a week, and gathered around us are my cousin Abel and his and Rosendo's father (my father's brother), my gray-complected Uncle Abel, looking considerably older than I remembered. It's my first time in Mexico City. I make sure they know we're married without parental blessing because my husband is my father's worst nightmare come alive: a Jew and even worse—a *socialist*. Compared to the Protestant Sundays of my New York childhood with its gray, deserted streets echoing to the funereal melancholy of the Riverside Church carillon, Mexico fairly explodes with color. Streetside stalls brim with vegetables and fruits and native crafts; women cram the markets, their baskets overflowing. Parents grip children by the hand, threading their way through the throngs. Youngsters dance in the streets and the sound of music vibrates everywhere. Blazing sunlight lifts the finials of colonial architecture in fine relief. Textiles and ceramics bear messages of a suppressed pre-Columbian past. Churches squat on the ruins of ancient pyramids, their sedate baroque proportions marked by unruly indigenous signals trying to break through. But over the next four weeks, the words I manage in Spanish—a language that remains awkward for me to this day—bends my tongue, and even though my courage grows, I experience a certain psychic turmoil when I try to speak it.

When I ask to see the Mexico City house with the carriage entrance where my father was supposed to have lived with a pony, five parrots, and a cat and dog, my cousins laugh. It seems not to exist. Instead Rosendo makes sure we see the sights, daylong excursions to Teotihuacan and Chapultepec, home of Emperor Maximilian and Empress Carlota during the French occupation. I still remember it, a Sunday toward the end of May, the museum filled with ornate imperial memorabilia, but what stays with me to this day is the throng of families crowding the exhibits: barefoot Indian women, nursing their wee children under their rebozos, accompanied by men in sombreros, homespun clothing, and huaraches, awed by the solid malachite urns and the opulence of a patrimony that would forever stay beyond their reach.

On our last day, we attend a turn-of-the-century theater. My eyes scan the plush upholstery, the elaborate balconies, the secluded box seats where I imagine my father as a tiny boy, dressed in the short velvet pants and lace collar of his era, his short legs stretched straight in front of him, his small feet shod in high button shoes, waiting for the scarlet velvet curtains to inch open, revealing the magic of a puppet stage. I wonder what had happened to this little boy to turn him into the sad and dour man I have come to know.

Back home from Mexico, estranged or not, I must have hoped to legitimize my choice by letting my family know I had married. I rode the subway from our home in Brooklyn to Manhattan's Upper West Side alone. There was no need to subject my husband to what I had good reason to suspect might turn into an uproar.

As my mother served lunch she spared us her usual "he who does not work shall not eat." We sat at the pea-green utility table where we had taken our meals together from the time I rebelled, no longer willing to sit at my child's table. Perhaps my parents were anxious. After all, I had not been home in nearly two years. My father let me know that when my alma mater came calling offering me a theater arts instructorship, he told them he wouldn't know how to find me.

Throughout the meal my parents hid behind a wall of words until at last they grew silent as my mother served dessert.

"I imagine you want to know why I came to see you today?"

The dessert spoon hung immobile in her hand. Silence spread over the table like a stain. I said what I'd prepared to say. At the very mention of my husband's name my father leaped up, enraged, from his chair, but from where I sat I had the advantage. As I raced down the corridor, I could hear my mother trying to hold him back. "Emilio, Emilio," she shouted, "No matter what she's done, she's still my daughter."

It was the stuff of farce, but the divide had long been crossed. It would be the last time I would see my father in life, the last time he would try to lay a violent hand on me. When I reached the street, I was too out of breath, too stunned to feel anything but relief. I knew I would never be back. I wouldn't have to listen any longer to what my parents had to say about the man I'd married. I said goodbye to the house of hate for good, although years of recurring nightmares tossed me back there, still a prisoner of my past. It would take me a lifetime to come full circle, able at last to revisit that past, there to uncover the roots that, consciously and otherwise, have made me what I am.

5. Marking Time: Bottle Washer

In those early years, our income from my husband's internship wouldn't begin to meet our expenses. It seemed quite natural for me to go to work, something I had gotten used to from the age of fourteen. So began my inglorious working history, which in the telling seems more like an string of pratfalls. But without quite realizing it, my apparently aimless choices of employment provided me with some of the skills I would come to depend on when I settled on a life's work at last, though at the time exactly what that might be was still a matter of conjecture. Meanwhile, I was buying time. I could defer the moment when I would have to declare myself.

In pre-internet days, the New York labor force relied on the one-inch-thick, gender-segregated want ad section of the *New York Times*. My English major—my presumed social security for life—qualified me for the many challenging life choices available to women in the fifties: receptionist, "girl Friday," PBX operator, file clerk, or office assistant.

Throughout those early years of survival employment, I observed the patterns of racial and gender discrimination that characterized the U.S. labor market. An opening at MetLife provided one of the more memorable interviews. With her frilly blouse and demure gold cross dangling on a chain around her neck, the personnel manager could have been a nun in recovery. She studied my application, noted my married prefix. After the usual questions, she came to the crux of the matter: did I plan on getting pregnant any time soon? There was no way I wanted work at MetLife—or get pregnant for that matter—but grabbing the bait was entirely too appealing. "I thought you were interested in hiring my time, not my body." The cheekiness of my reply didn't stop her trying to sell me on the features of the Christmas Club, in which a provident MetLife set aside a portion from each paycheck to ensure all its employees got to keep the economy chugging with sufficient funds to buy presents at year's end. In the interim, MetLife could compound the interest—a leg up she forgot to mention.

If I was going to become our breadwinner, I decided I needed to please myself. Accordingly, when I dropped in at the personnel offices of *Time* magazine, my stint at Barnard College was the open sesame. I was hired on the spot—as a copy clerk. The challenges of this position required posting—by hand—all editorial changes on some seven copies of all stories passing through the copy desk, by the assistant editor, the editor, the "researchers," and the production and photography departments among others, and then redistributing each of the seven copies back. It bemused me why a degree was required to fulfill such onerous responsibilities, but *Time* provided plenty of grist for my apprenticeship as a social scientist. One day a gentleman of somewhat mature age stumped past the copy desk. "That's Henry Luce," someone whispered, awestruck. "Who's Henry Luce?" I was unimpressed. My coworker quickly set me straight. *Time* was Henry Luce's fiefdom, and the "fringes" proved it. Should an employee seek self-improvement, college and graduate school courses were at corporate expense. Should the anxieties of the job prove taxing, psychiatric care was fully compensated. (I could relate to that one.) Should a female employee give birth, the family received a silver loving cup engraved with the child's name, signed by Henry Luce, and a six-month-long maternity leave. New fathers were out of luck.

Without being quite aware of it at first, I had entered a patriarchal world, an exclusively white enclave governed by strict hierarchy. All editors, photographers, and writers held one qualification in common: they were male. All typists and researchers were female. Barring sexual reassignment, no researcher could ever aspire to join the writing ranks. The researchers were housed in the corner offices, each of which was occupied by a central island of filing cabinets, positioned back to back. Their generous surfaces provided a convenient, eye-level location for case upon case of Johnnie Walker Red and Black. As Sunday evenings wore on, while the magazine was being put to bed, the sound of retching could be heard whenever the women's restroom doors swung open. That year, although the majority of staff, writers and researchers alike, backed Adlai Stevenson—along with Johnnie Walker—Henry Luce won: *Time* backed Eisenhower.

We had finally arranged our lives, Felix and I, to share a roof, yet every weekend as he walked in one door, red eyed from thirty-six straight hours of internship, I walked out the other to work for *Time*. Sometimes, weekends when he was not on duty, he met me at midnight Saturday nights to accompany me on the subway home. But after a while, crumbs from *Time*'s table or not, it didn't seem like the best way to run a marriage.

In 1943 George Papanicolaou, a cytologist and immigrant from Greece, copublished the book *Diagnosis of Uterine Cancer by the Vaginal Smear*, documenting his research findings dating back to 1928. But he and his colleague found serious problems obtaining backing until the Commonwealth Fund, a beneficiary of Harkness philanthropy, awarded them a princely grant of $1,800. The foundation considered their research highly speculative at the time, yet it was the Pap smear that would make the Commonwealth Fund famous. It was to the Commonwealth Fund I next applied.

Housed in a former Harkness mansion on East Sixty-Eighth Street, the Commonwealth Fund was located in a district richly suited to millionaires but hardly served by any plebian luncheon counters or public transportation. My duties there—mostly as a correspondence secretary—were not much more challenging than they had been at *Time*, but, starting with the interview, opportunities for the amateur social sleuth were spectacular. My prospective boss outlined my responsibilities before filling me in on Commonwealth

Fund culture. The top man occupying the director's chair was socialite and former Yaley football star Malcolm Aldrich, who coincidentally held a seat on the New York Stock Exchange. The normal hierarchy included staff people, secretaries (me), office assistants, and "the boys." He described these last as runners, or in more common usage, go-fers, variously aged between forty-five and sixty-five years. The out-of-the-way location of foundation headquarters necessitated a brown-bag company lunchroom. Offhandedly he mentioned "the boys" happened to be "colored." The staff occupied one table, the directors (male) another, secretaries (female) yet another. The "boys" had a table designated entirely to themselves.

"What would happen," I innocently asked, "if I were to join the boys for lunch?"

In my four-year-long history of survival employment, the Commonwealth Fund emerged as the only organization that employed any people of color in any capacity whatsoever. To this day it utterly astonishes me that it was foolish enough to hire me at all. The pratfall part took place one day in the lunchroom, where I dutifully joined the secretaries for lunch. Conversation meandered before it landed on pornography, when someone opined that the pope had the largest smut library in the world. Notwithstanding that my loyalties to the church had paled some time back, I felt obliged to point out that the curating agency was not so much the pope as the Vatican itself. At exactly 1:00 p.m., Malcolm Aldrich had me sweating on the carpet. He fired me on the spot. I felt devastated!

Putting my English major lifetime social security to the test, I fell back on Harper & Row, where the medical journal department hired me as a proofreader. The salary was microscopic, which I later discovered was standard policy for a company whose budget balanced on hiring as many disabled people as possible. ("Cheaper that way," the editor was reputed to have said.) I rose—still on a shoestring—to become assistant editor of the *Journal of Obstetrics and Gynecology*. Most medical school graduates have mastered writing fairly lucidly, but on those rare occasions when Harper & Row received a garbled submission, I parlayed the knowledge I'd first acquired from the Barnard pudendal charts. I had *Gray's Anatomy* at my elbow and a doctor-in-the-making in my bed. But it dawned on me that a working life spent in an office was not an ideal fit. Just up the subway line from Harper & Row, Hunter College offered the night classes required for the basic one-size-fits-all New York City teaching credential. I enrolled.

That summer, with an entire month off before my husband began his residency at the Brooklyn VA hospital, we planned to visit France. Harper & Row had other ideas. Two weeks' vacation was the national norm. I offered to forego a salary and take a leave of absence for weeks three and four; the nation—and Harper & Row—would have none of it, not even when I offered to work double time on my return. I resigned the day before we left for France.

Barely arrived in Paris, we boarded the sleeper Train Bleu, destination the Riviera, with its antiquated couches and its quaint fold-out chamber pots. Quite by happenstance, we discovered Cap-d'Ail, in those days still a separate municipality. All morning we sat on the rocks bordering the Mediterranean, stunned by its dizzying blue and the dark vermilion rocks of its shoreline. Clambering over them, perhaps because I was wearing espadrilles, must have made me lose my footing. Helpful citizens directed us to a street clinic where I got bandaged up, but when the staff discovered we hailed from l'Amerique, there was no damping their enthusiasm. Had they been able, they would have perched us on their shoulders. All along the Avenue du Trois Septembre, as far as the eye could see, the Stars and Stripes flew along with the tricolor. Our guides swept us inside the small town hall, where city officials made much of us. This was V-E Day 1958, when U.S. cred—in Europe at least—was still running high.

Under the immense skies of Burgundy, we discovered its Romanesque churches, one of them featuring quaint capitals by a carver, whose name, still then unnoticed, appeared hidden in plain sight on the tympanum above the Autun Cathedral doors: *Gislebertus hoc fecit*.* But it was our ramble through the golden light of Provence and the Languedoc country, marveling at its noontime play in those few Romanesque cloisters still surviving wars, and Rockefeller's art dealers that most warmed my heart, places like Saint Trophime at Ar-

---

* "Gilbert made this." Everyone read Latin in the Middle Ages—everyone who could read, which conveniently excluded the feudal equivalent of the 99 percent.

les, Fontfoide (with its black Madonna) in the eastern Pyrenees, and most exquisitely of all, the cloister Saint-Rémy-de-Provence where Vincent spent some of his last, mad, tortured months.

But that first trip to France surprised me with a gift unannounced: at the Theater Festival of Avignon, I took in my first performance cast in the idiom I would later claim as my own, in which the company collaborated with designers, conceptual artists, poets, and musicians to develop an event, instead of merely putting on a play.

On our return to Paris we roamed the streets of the Marais in the company of my husband's friends. Jewish survivors, all of them, of the German occupation, who pointed out the bookstore, still the flagship of one of France's prominent publishers, that carried door signs during the war reading "Forbidden to dogs and Jews," and the sites where Jews had been rounded up for deportation first to the Vel d'Hiver, the winter hippodrome, later on to Drancy, road stop on the way to Auschwitz.

Their base at that time was still a tenement on Rue de la Butte-aux-Cuailles (nostalgically referred to as La Butte). In the sixteenth-century Paris of Henri IV, that same hill was wild country where the king and his retinue hunted quail, but now it held a tumbling-down building dating from the nineteenth century with its tenement bathrooms, one to each floor, with an open pit referred to as a crocodile after its scored footrests. Yesterday's paper supplied the bathroom tissue. But what it may have lacked in amenities, it compensated in spiritual dimension. The family matriarch everyone affectionately called Mamie came from a long, distinguished line of Polish rabbis. The war had torn her Polish husband—who had hoped to make a better life in Paris as a rag-and-bone man—from the family, sending him first to Drancy and then to Auschwitz, where he met his death, along with members of their extended family, many of them little children. Mamie, who lived *contente* to be a hundred, kept the family's history in her head. She held everyone close in her great heart, all those who returned and the many who never came back.

6. Chief Cook

The United States we returned to was in the grip of a serious recession. Still in survival job mode, it would be some time before I could score an interview at the National Conference of Christians and Jews. Their headquarters were located on Fifty-Seventh Street just west of Fifth Avenue on the first floor in a highly trafficked area. I don't remember a job description, nor do I remember anything resembling a job because the boss I was supposed to report to existed in absentia. It took me some time to discover that his lost weekends stretched to include Mondays through Fridays. Because the staff was unswervingly monochrome, there was scant opportunity to further any amateur social sleuthing except by hearsay. In the entryway, prominently displayed on an easel, and highly visible from a window on the street, sat an impressively large portrait of contralto Marian Anderson, the first person of color to break through the Met's velvet curtain. But it was a portrait that enjoyed certain magic properties. Among NCCJ's most lavish donors was a gaggle of Texas oilmen. Shortly before they appeared on the scene, the portrait of Marian Anderson disappeared behind a closet door.

When Hunter College awarded me the one-size-fits-all credential licensing me to teach, my pratfall days came to an end. An all-girls Brooklyn high school hired me to teach English for one semester. For the first time in my working life, I felt fully engaged doing meaningful work, perhaps too fully engaged. I quickly recognized the advantages to be had—and not just for students—of not requiring any homework; otherwise, with thirty-five students to a class, four classes a day, I would have had to correct 140 writing assignments every single night, including weekends.

There was a more serious problem: at twenty-six years of age, my appearance suggested I'd barely survived puberty; compared with me, most of my students looked remarkably zaftig. I took to solving my lagging developmental problems with an upsweep hairstyle and a spinsterly chignon. But try as I might, as I wrote my name on the board on the first day of class, I could hear a rumble of remarks:

"Hey. She da teach?"

"Dunno."

"Yeah."

"Hunh?"

"Yeah. She's da teach."

I imagined that in terms of discipline, compared to a coed school, all-girls might be less challenging, but happily, although I never concerned myself overly much with keeping order, it provided abundant opportunities for social research. Each class had its own personality, each challenging in its own way. The great majority of my students were the daughters of Italian longshoremen. On one class roster, student IQs registered at a mean of sixty-six. I soon discovered there was nothing deficient with their cognitive smarts. All had no problem interacting with me. All were keen observers of the social scene. The class was racially mixed. It was supposed to be a "slow learner" catch-all to which I became social consultant.

"My boyfriend is two-timing me. Mrs. Leneman, is that jive?"

I said I thought it was—but not if she was jiving him.

"Woffo we gotta read *Ivanhoe*?"

My student had a point. If reading *Ivanhoe* was inappropriate in the Fifth Avenue former McCormick mansion of my high school days, where I balked at its door-stopping properties, it was yet more unsuited to this student population.

Although my chairperson was reluctant to make any concession, from the list of approved texts I was allowed to choose a substitute, Steinbeck's *The Pearl*. Despite my sense of its inauthenticity (the much more authentic narrative by Tomás Rivera, *And the Earth Did Not Swal-*

low Him, would not be published until 1971), I considered that my students might better be able to relate to its milieu than they might to a course of medieval castles and jousts. To check up on their reading assignments, I announced a spot quiz requiring one-word answers. Most students performed well. One student, a Native American, who always sat in the back row invisibilizing herself, handed in her quiz results. For each one-word answer she had drawn a small icon, a hieroglyphic answer, every one correct. Paulo Freire's work *Pedagogy of the Oppressed* would appear ten years later, but my own past had taught me this was not a person with an IQ of sixty-six. She must be singled out, and her unique abilities reenforced. I wasted no time pointing out to her not only that her answers were correct but that she had actually invented a writing system similar to that found on some Native American petroglyphs. I don't know what became of her, but I hope she kept the lesson warm in her heart.

I had one class, however, that agreed, tacitly or otherwise, to break my spirit. They were tough and unconceding. Sometimes their surly expressions had me close to tears. There seemed to be nothing I could do to establish a culture of trust, let alone the easy give and take without which learning is impossible. Thank goodness it was sex that broke the impasse. I no longer remember what short story we read, but it certainly greased the skids, attributing to what is a basic human act all kinds of meaning overlays. They warmed to participation-by-poll. "How many think sex is jive? How many think sex means love?" We followed it with a serious discussion of human relations. Discussion was still raging when the bell rang, signaling a ceasefire had been declared. Angela, a dreamy Italian girl, wrote several authentic, remarkably poignant short stories. I approached my chairperson wondering if perhaps she might be placed in a gifted class. My chair waved a dismissive hand.

"She probably copied them."

My most energetic class held a surprise for me. The curriculum assigned *A Midsummer Night's Dream*. It was territory I knew well from the time our small girls' tongues stumbled over Peaseblossom and Mustardseed in the light of Giffy's kerosene lamp. But how to make it real to girls whose ferocious quarrels I broke up in the school corridors? Who were streetwise and not averse to street fighting after school let out? Why not translate Shakespeare into the language of the street? Hermia and Helena could just as well indulge in a mano a mano over Demetrius. (Some years later, Peter Brooke's company would tap a similarly rowdy vein.)

"I'll tear your eyes out!"

"Bitch, leggo my hair!"

My students understood that kind of language, they made use of it quite frequently—and it gratified my own thwarted theatrical aspirations.

An ongoing New York newspaper strike kept me in the dark that week, but my students knew what was on. They had no reason to rely on fuddy-duddy things like newspapers. A TV broadcast of *Midsummer's Night's Dream* happened to run. At first I had no idea why they were mobbing me in class next day, until before my astonished eyes, they got to hamming up some of the scenes.

In my racially mixed slow-learner class, the girls, condemned because of their paper IQ scores, discovered *The Diary of Anne Frank*. They were roughly the same age as Anne. Despite the controversy surrounding its provenance—a problem that escaped me at the time—it was a curriculum choice I made because I suspected they would relate to it. We finished the book. There was a feeling of sadness in the room. "Could you give us another one just like it?" But alas! I could not. Although millions had gone to their deaths, there was only one Anne Frank, but they had learned to read and with it they had learned to write, and if they ever had to take another IQ test, I hoped their old records could be expunged.

By then I had grasped the futility of trying to move the mountains of the New York school system's bureaucracy. At best, I may have reduced it to mole hills by learning—to some degree at least—to hold my tongue. I even scored a measure of approval when my colleagues admitted that at the start they had thoroughly resented my attitude because I arrived too starry eyed and "fresh as paint." My silence convinced them that I was safe now, that I had settled for the regulation breaststroke that kept them punching the time clock and drawing their salaries year after year.

As the semester wound to a close, we discovered I was pregnant.

I considered that that new life was somehow teaching me—about to teach me something for which I considered myself woefully unprepared. My journal at the time reads: "I hope that when my time comes, I will have put not one but two people into the world." That tailcoat rider was myself. But I had no time to worry. My 140 students saw to that.

Although—predictably—my one-semester contract was not renewed, we were unconcerned. We had enough saved up to tide us over till we left for South Carolina where Felix would discharge his two years of military service at Charleston's Naval Hospital. But with newfound leisure on my hands I had time to think. To reconnect with my deep anxieties. I had time to consider that, with my dysfunctional family background, I knew nothing or very little about birthing babies, nothing or very little about raising them. Even scarier, given my deep ambivalence toward my mother, I feared a pregnancy that might trap me into a similarly limited existence. And something buried even deeper began to haunt me: how could someone without any sense of her beginnings ever hope for any generational continuity?

I trembled like a dog. Psychotherapy was hardly within our means. If I obeyed my notion that I needed to seek some form of help for my feelings of terror, I knew the only possible resource must be a public facility or clinic. But my clumsy brush with an old therapist holdover from the Freudian school of female hysteria guaranteed I would not be back any time soon. All he seemed to want to discuss was my sex life. Once again I deferred the moment I would have to do the difficult work of revisiting my past. For now, pregnant or not, I wanted a life, one I could live fully without looking back.

Day Four

What brought Jean Blum to the attention of the press was her discovery—the first reported one—of a disappearance in immigrant detention.

The death of Ahmad Tanveer is of unusual significance because the immigration authorities could produce no record that Tanveer had ever been detained in the first place, let alone that he had died in their custody. Without the intervention of Jean Blum, this incident might never have come to light. Tom Jawetz of the ACLU reflected on the troubling aspects of this particular case: "We still do not know and we cannot know if there are other deaths that have never been disclosed by ICE or that ICE itself knows nothing about." Congresswoman Zoe Lofgren, pleading the necessity for greater accountability to Congress, wondered if failure to report this death reflected carelessness or "something more sinister."

Said the New York Times (April 3, 2009): "The difficulty of confirming Ahmad [Tanveer]'s very existence shows that death could fall between the cracks in immigration detention."

Jean Blum is very clear: "Although immigrant detainees are arrested and held by Immigration and Customs Enforcement (ICE) under the aegis of the Department of Homeland Security, it is important to understand they are not criminals, they are people who work hard, many of them heads of families, trying to better themselves, striving for their piece of the American dream, as all of us did," she reminds me. She continues:

> Many of them will be deported anyway for past misdemeanors such as having a broken tail light, or not paying tax on a packet of cigarettes because they are being held in "administrative detention," a provision of the Illegal Immigrant and Immigrant Responsibility (IIRIRA) Act of 1996 which under Title III denies them the right of appeal such that they can be removed without judicial oversight.
>
> Under the U.S. Constitution, not only citizens, but all persons are accorded the right to defend themselves before a court of law, under the provisions of "administrative detention," an entire group of people—mostly poor and almost all persons of color—has been denied that right. . . . The entire ICE operation is in violation of the U.S. Constitution. Not only does "administrative detention" establish and perpetuate a dangerous parallel and unconstitutional system of punishment, once the law is compromised, it may be used to apply to any other demographic group.

Toward the conclusion of our ten days together, Jean shared with me the archive she had taken pains to deposit in a secret location where the Paterson Police Department would never be able to unearth or destroy it. We spent our last day Xeroxing selected excerpts, I operating the machine, she collating, a task that kept us working until the shop announced its closing.

In the Charleston Naval Hospital's delivery room, on the assumption that a gassed patient is a happy patient, I've been drugged with a mouthful of gas. In my semiconscious state, a nurse's voice goes off like a gun.

"*You have a boy!*"

I hear our son wailing vigorously, a sign he's come into the world all cylinders primed. Reassured, I raise myself on one elbow. "I want to see the placenta." My words are not so slurred from anesthesia I can't make my meaning plain. After all, how many women are ever permitted to see a placenta, any placenta, let alone their own? An attending obligingly produces a white enamel pan. In it rests something closely resembling a slab of liver. He flips it over. My side, my son's side, but my nice white lady cred is shot: I have my husband's word for it. He's at my side at the delivery table. He's heard his colleague's sharp intake of breath. This is Charleston, home of beguiling but submissive women. Women like that know better than to ask to see a placenta. A nurse brings me my son wrapped up so tight he looks like a giant chrysalis. She places him on my abdomen. Blissed out, I collapse into the best sleep I've ever enjoyed.

Next day I write in my journal:

> The hour is early morning. The August sun floods the room in gentle light. As I prop myself up in bed I catch sight of the dust bunnies lurking under the unoccupied bed alongside mine. This is the Naval Hospital where just this year three babies die of post natal infections because of poor sanitation.
>
> Footsteps approach in the hallway. A nurse appears, a small bundle in her arms. She places my son on the bed beside me. She urges me to unwrap him, so small, so helpless I'm scared to touch him. At last, I take him in my arms. this small being who was living inside my own body only yesterday.

Like death, birth separates us from the dailiness of living to allow for one breathtaking moment, a brief glimpse of the profoundly unexplained. Why here, and now? Why who or what? Why in this consciousness, and not another? Why here on this planet? Why in this form? With prehensile hands, destined to walk upright? Why not somewhere else in this universe, or in another of what may be its many generations? Why anything at all?

My mother-in-law takes two weeks off from her New York medical practice to help out. On my third day postpartum, Felix brings her along as he fetches us home. I carry our son into the house. It's barely cool inside, though the air conditioner is going full tilt. As I bend over just enough to lower him into his baby carriage, I flush out a cockroach bigger than a baby's fist. I begin to cry. My husband puts Beethoven's *Pastoral Symphony* on the turntable. I cry all afternoon. My mother-in-law serves dinner. "Before you say something sentimental, just eat your soup," she admonishes me. But the tide will not be stemmed.

I cry for five days, but are they tears of pain? Or tears of joy? Some logjam deep within has broken, something deeply buried. It's as if inside there's a great melting of some kind of psychic ice. Sheets of it slough off. What have I held inside so tightly that now it's taking a dam-burst to break up? What is it? Something absent so long I have forgotten if it ever had a name. Some kind of peace. It's as if I'd held to some belief that I was somehow condemned from the beginning, condemned by the absence of my own history never to engender anything life giving. And yet here is proof! I have brought life into the world! Something miraculous has come of my body. Me. It's as if until now, I haven't known I had a body, a procreating body.

I don't share my feelings with my mother-in-law. I know she means well, but I don't expect her to understand. She's practical. She helps me cook and attend to routine household chores. And she loves babies. She shows me how to set the proper water temperature (it should equal that of the womb) to bathe my son, how to lower him very gradually into the bathwater so the watery element doesn't shock him, and how to bathe his infinitesimally small body, to hold his tiny head cradled in my left hand while I soap and rinse him with my right. She shows me how to lift him out of the water and lay him on his receiving blanket to pat him dry, how to slather him thoroughly with oil, before dusting him with powder, head to toe. When she's done he's more thoroughly coated than a drumstick ready for the pan. I smile gratefully but I know I won't be doing it quite this way once she's gone. Meanwhile, all four gas burners are turned up maximum to ensure the baby won't catch cold. It's August in Charleston, and the sweat nearly blinds me. In our living room, the air conditioner grinds on day and night, helping us battle the heat, though we wage a losing war against what Charlestonians euphemistically refer to as palmetto beetles, the two-inch-long cockroaches we stomp without pity and brush off our naked bodies when they kamikaze us in the shower.

We're about to sample Bull Connor's South firsthand, Bull Connor, the Montgomery sheriff who will set his dogs against black demonstrators in 1963. Public water fountains so canny they can distinguish between "white" and "colored." And canny public restrooms and canny beaches. The ocean itself would be assigned if posts could be sunk in it, but water is a fluid, more receiving element. I observe all this through knowledgeable eyes: my early education at the hands of socialist-inclined nuns had us debating segregation as early as 1946—for a full year.

We are a one-wage-earning family now. I can luxuriate as a stay-at-home mom, except I have a hungry baby to feed, baby bottles to wash, a soiled baby to change, a tired baby to rock, and diapers and washing to hang out, and dinner to cook, and breakfast to make and shopping at the PX once a week and palmetto beetles to stomp. But I don't have to board any rattletrap bus at 5:00 a.m. like my one-day-a-week black cleaning helper who takes up the slack that normally would be mine. All the same, l feel uncomfortable, as though I am not doing enough. Under the surface of things, my mother's Thessalonians keep carping. It doesn't help that she keeps parcel posting me snoods, this despite Charleston's subtropical heat, to hide hair that *still* won't curl like Shirley Temple's hair.

My helper's name is Emiline. Nearly six feet tall, she favors ballerina skirts, bouffant petticoats, and dancing slippers to trudge through the predawn fields, catching the bus to clean our houses, mine and my neighbors'. We pay her Yankee-scale wages and gift her with two chickens from the PX every week. On the one occasion when—for some unremembered reason—she misses the bus home, we drive her deep into the countryside. The road winds through South Carolina's pine forests and along the red soil of its unpaved roads.

"It's here," she says. Here is a tongue and groove one-room shack, blackened with age. The porch roof sags; the posts are out of plumb. There are no chairs out front. Her little boy, Freddie, skylarks in the yard. His grandma minds him all day while Emiline is at work. With no man in the house, she's the sole support. We all get together, I and my neighbors, at Christmastime to buy Freddie a red tricycle. But debating segregation is one thing; seeing it in action quite another. No matter how sympathetic we are, there is no way in our white privilege, no way at all for us to know what it's like to walk in black moccasins, even for one day. Passersby that lynch with their eyes. Beatings casually administered for sitting in the wrong seat. Refusal of restaurant, even diner service, the barring of hotel lodging for a night, permission to bleed to death at the hospital gates because it's staked out for whites only. And the dogs.

It's the end of January, spring in Charleston. The azalea gardens erupt in vibrant color. My mother-in-law is visiting. We make plans to visit the gardens come the weekend. I'll put David down for his nap in the morning. We'll leave just after noon. But she and Felix linger over the lunch table. I don't feel particularly included when their conversation turns to medicine. Instead, I busy myself getting us ready. Packing diapers and baby bottles in a carryall. They're still talking. So as not to rush them, I decide I might as well not let the crusting dishes wait. I'm soaping a glass salad bowl when it slips, I make to catch it. A shard stabs me in the wrist. I see my arm dissected, the fatty tissue exposed, yellow as tallow. The good news is the artery is not severed. The bad news is it's my dominant side.

We've traded red azaleas for red puddles on the floor, which my mother-in-law scurries about wiping up with a washcloth. We will not see the Charleston gardens today. Fortunately, the hand surgeon is on call. I'm in the OR in no time; a local block anesthesia numbs my hand. The surgeon gets to work, resecting half my tendons. A certain hand movement will be impossible from now on; what that means is that from the age of twenty-eight, the fingers of my right hand will appear to be deformed and the tips of certain fingers will always be devoid of sensation. The surgery is over rather quickly. Stitches are applied. My hand is immobilized in a cast that makes my elevated lower arm and hand look like a pompous goose. The surgeon swings by for a final look. "You'll never play the piano again," is his matter-of-fact assessment. It's February 1, 1960, the date of the famed Greensboro luncheon sit-in, the first of many. But for now, Charleston stays quiet.

A Mrs. Williams comes to lend a hand, cooking for us, dressing me, combing my hair, changing our son. We are a rare sight, the two of us, talking amicably together in Hampton Park as she pushes David's baby carriage. Such public fraternizing is not the norm in Charleston. Mrs. Williams goes to church. She's in touch with the NAACP. Her ear is to the ground. Although some weeks ago the Greensboro sitters had been met with insults and beatings, with immense courage they stuck to their pledge of nonviolence. Charleston still seems to be asleep, but something is brewing. Mrs. Williams isn't sure just what or maybe she's not telling.

Two months later, I can fasten a diaper with one hand, and on April 1 twenty-four black students from Charleston's Burke High School march into Kress department store on King Street; the women wear hats and gloves, the men suits. They sit down at the lunch counter and refuse to leave. Eventually they are arrested for trespassing. The civil rights movement has begun. It will open the way for other people of color: the Asians and the Mexicans. It will reach its climax in 1963 with the Birmingham protests. Bull Connor will unleash his water cannons. Led by Martin Luther King Jr., the people will cross the Edmund Pettus Bridge with immense courage, aware of glowering police and the mayhem awaiting them and their little children.

Our stint in Charleston is drawing to a close. We will see none of this fear. But our two years of living as a one-income family show me it's possible to slow down, and among other things, to consider what it means to live with segregation. To my way of thinking, the Civil War is still being fought and will always be fought as long as the terms of surrender leave a people humiliated, much as the terms of surrender after World War I humiliated a people. It's the kind of affront nearly impossible for a defeated people to forget. And, as German World War II history has shown, taking such residual feelings out on people of a minority race is never without ugly consequence.

With no Truth and Reconciliation Commission, no opportunity publicly to exorcise its guilt about the crimes of slavery as it was practiced on the rice and indigo and cotton plantations, a few of which we've visited during our stay, the South will find it historically impossible *to forgive the very people on whom it has visited such cruelty*, let alone embrace them. Tragedy requires redemption before it can be let go. There has been no such catharsis in the South.

And I have the leisure to reflect on the satisfactions—and the challenges—of domestic life, and how leaving the secrets of one's birth unexamined is like mortgaging the past while hoping to live an untroubled future. It means that I will leave undone the work of coming to terms with the setbacks of my childhood. But life is good, we're happy together, our days filled with the joys of raising a small child. We will be making our new life, not in the Bronx as we initially planned, but thanks to friends who've sold us on the Bay Area, we'll be heading west. Why face the grim legacies of childhood when the opportunity comes to leave them three thousand miles behind?

7. San Francisco Story

In terms of dumb luck, our settling in San Francisco rates a ten. Although more spread out than New York, it's much more easily navigated—if one has access to a car—a consideration that will count for something when the time comes to declare myself. In the intervening six years of unrelieved domesticity, at best I find only occasional relief. When it crops up, it's mostly connected with music, playing continuo with a roving baroque music ensemble that meets weekly, accompanying my husband and our friends either on piano or harpsichord, or producing music, raising funds for the Jewish day school my sons attend, organizing three successful concerts featuring recognized musicians.

If I resorted during those years to "taking courses," normally the refuge of bored housewives, it was not only because friends were doing the same. It came with a dawning realization that, as things stood, I was beginning to find life at home not entirely satisfying.

Day Five

One element characterizing most societies consists of a process of initiation. Does the U.S. process, consisting of cruel and unusual punishment, reflect the dark side of its collective persona? And can that dark side ever be reformed? Not so long as the wanton arrest of citizens and noncitizens alike enriches those privately and publicly held corporations that benefit.

In 2009 I wrote:

> All detention facilities, public and private, enter into a contractual agreement with the Department of Homeland Security/ICE to house detainees. It is in their interest to obtain the most favorable rate per diem while keeping their overhead low. This they accomplish by overcrowding, by providing inadequate diet and poor-to-nonexistent medical attention, and by keeping staff salaries and training to a minimum, resulting in the kinds of prison abuse both verbal and physical, documented earlier. In 2003, at $28,000 per inmate/year plus a 10% commissary markup, housing detainees brought in $12 million to the Passaic County Jail which, according to the sheriff's department spokesperson, passed directly into the county general fund.

County and Federally run jails are now in competition with privately run facilities, of which the numbers rose from 5 in 1990 to over 200 by 2000, But if evidence serves, compared to publicly run facilities, privately operated facilities such as those run by ... CoreCivic (formerly known as Corrections Corporation of America) with 63 facilities in 19 states, compete to bring their overhead even lower. To secure a profitable bottom line, CoreCivic lobbies a compliant congress for stricter detention rules; it secures its interests through the use of interlocking directorates, political contributions, and expensive lobbying; to head key projects, it hires retired government administrators and military personnel who'll guarantee results.

ICE operates twenty-four regional field offices, staffed with more than twenty thousand "agents." Because of its covert character, lack of oversight allows it to operate in a culture of impunity, leading to the runaway cruelty and corruption we see today.

As of March 2018, 71 percent of immigrant detention beds were contracted by private prison companies, the two largest being CoreCivic and the GEO Group (formerly known as Wackenhut). ICE's budget nearly doubled from $3.3 billion in 2003 to $6.1 billion in 2016. It has increased under the "no tolerance" policy of the present administration to $7.3 billion in 2018 and a projected $8.3 billion in 2019.

According to a 2017 estimate, the GEO Group and CoreCivic operate fifty-one thousand detention beds in a network of at least 637 facilities. In 2018 more than $3.6 billion of the U.S. budget is spent on immigrant detention in nonprofit as well as private, for-profit jails and prisons, a billion-dollar increase from 2017, which reflects the boom in immigrant detention during this administration's second year in office. And it has recently come to light that ICE has placed in its custody four thousand more people than Congress funded. Earlier in 2018, faced with a similar shortfall, the Department of Homeland Security, which oversees ICE, quietly reallocated to ICE funds it had originally earmarked for FEMA, this when half of Puerto Rico remains without electricity following Hurricane Maria. What is yet more alarming is that following the administration's zero-tolerance orders, plans are currently underway to "retrofit" military installations close to the border including Goodfellow Air Force Base, Fort Bliss Air Force Base, Little Rock Air Force Base, the U.S. Navy's Wolf and Silverhill Outlying Fields, and Camp Pendleton to house up to two hundred thousand immigrants in concentration camps, twenty-five thousand of them in a hurricane-prone area with no plans for emergency evacuation.

The GEO Group earned more than $2.26 billion from housing more than 600,000 detainees in its detention centers and prisons. After the 2016 election, its stock price ballooned 81 percent. The CEO of Southwest Key Programs, a "nonprofit" private prison company operating facilities housing up to 11,900 detained migrant children, hauled in $1.5 million that year in salaries alone. And to increase their profits, private, for-profit prison corporations are happy to grease the skids. Before the 2016 elections, the GEO Group gave nearly $500,000 to a Republican super PAC and CoreCivic popped $250,000 to add splash to the 2017 inauguration's fanfare.

I enjoy one year of part-time employment managing my husband's office until fastening the buttons on my lab coat turns into a stretch. This time, thanks to natural childbirth and a handheld mirror, I participate in the birth of our son and get to fully experience the wonder and the overwhelming joy of giving birth, a feeling so intense I yield to the urge to call home—one last time perhaps—to let my parents in on the coming of their second grandchild. My father picks up the phone. "Just a minute," his voice sounds gray, "I'll call your mother," he says, dropping the receiver. A year later, my mother calls with news of his fatal heart attack. Her parting shot does little to invite me home for the funeral. "You killed him," she observes as she hangs up.

Things begin looking up. I don't know it yet, but the theater is silently sneaking up on me, about to reclaim me. Responding to a call for a home visit, my husband becomes a kind of in-house doctor to the San Francisco Mime Troupe. Its director, Ronnie Davis (or RGD as he styles himself) has a cultural vision that makes theater a political vehicle. The troupe's work attracts widening circles of dancers, musical and visual artists, and political theorists, people like Peter Berg, Jane Lapiner, Peter Solomon, Luis Valdez, Juris Swendsen, Pauline Oliveros, and activists like Emmett Grogan, founder of San Francisco's Diggers, and others who find themselves drawn to the troupe's politics and its rowdy theater style.

As "resident" physician, my husband is invited with me to attend one of the troupe's very first productions (1965), Bertolt Brecht's *The Exception and the Rule*. A memorable mise-en-scène features a prologue delivered by two women circling the stage, costumed in cat suits, muttering the opening lines in German.

Shortly thereafter, the troupe adopts the broad gestures of the Italian seventeenth- to eighteenth-century commedia as the vehicle best suited to project its political message in the parks around San Francisco, venues where it customarily performs. The style is familiar to me from the time I rescued Mayenne's crumbling first edition of *The Italian Comedy*, Pierre Louis Duchartre's seminal work, from her toss-out pile. That August, the troupe stages *Il Candelaio*, based on a commedia by Giordano Bruno.* Its raw nature has the National Park Service up in arms. Although 366 years have elapsed since Bruno was burned at the stake, its directors vote to revoke the company's performance permit on obscenity grounds. Litigation follows. Money must be raised to defray legal costs. I open our home to the troupe, serve up my signature Spanish paella, enough for all

---

* Giordano Bruno was burned at the stake in 1600 for insisting that the universe was infinite, that stars were distant suns, and that their planets might even foster life! It didn't help that his disposition was terminally cranky.

hands, while plotting with then-manager Bill Graham how best to raise funds.

We decide on a benefit rock concert in the troupe's Howard Street loft. It will feature the Mothers, Jefferson Airplane, and the John Handy Quartet, among others, the second rock extravaganza ever to be produced in San Francisco. In my mini skirt and flamboyant tights, I hawk orange juice and lab alcohol screwdrivers at twenty-five cents a pop. As the evening wears on and the temperature soars, I hang out the window for a breath of air to discover more than two thousand people massed along Howard Street, hoping to crash. One young buck from Stanford actually scales up the elevator shaft, watch fob and three-piece suit intact. At midnight, the fire department arrives to thin out the festivities. Thanks to that evening, the Fillmore West is born, and, to my husband's deep distress, rock 'n' roll blasts into my life and cannonballs me into a world of almost unlimited possibilities.

Director and San Francisco Mime Troupe lead actress Sandra Archer invites me to the troupe's Sunday morning commedia workshop. Fourteen years away from my undergraduate acting days have me paralyzed. Huddled in the troupe's unheated loft, shivering in my cheap polyester matron's coat, I sit glued to a repurposed pew, watching nothing like a religious observance. The next Sunday, still huddled in that coat, I watch an improvisation unfold based on a scenario RGD brings to the workshop. On stage the actors corner themselves into an impasse. Only some kind of catalyst can spring the action forward. In a flash, I'm running on stage, shedding my polyester and my housewife's life on the way.

From that day's improvisation, the season's offering, *Olive Pits*, based on a play by the sixteenth-century Spanish playwright Lope de Rueda, was born, and shedding my matron's life and coat, I allow myself the freedom to improvise with Peter Cohon (later Coyote), Luis Valdez (later of the Teatro Campesino) and Rob Hurwitt (later prominent San Francisco theater critic) among all the other mime troupe heavies. Wildly presentational, funky, improvisational, rebellious, intellectual—a style that lent a political voice to the heart of the sixties counterculture—the San Francisco Mime Troupe becomes home.

Until then, if I felt anything at all, it had been as someone's mother, or someone's wife, but without quite realizing it, the delay of marriage and housekeeping and, most critically, its financial support helped me recover a connection to my own first impulses. One day, quite without premeditation, I resurrected that polyester coat to sit by the front door, not quite able to initiate my own escape but unable to return upstairs. In time I made the transition—as so many women of previous generations failed to do—but if I managed it at all, it was not without help. My therapist was to find a point of access that, much later, would become a benchmark of my own teaching. "What do you love?" he asked me. My answer was telling: "To look," as if I had become so peripheral to any aspect of public life, all I could do was witness it. Although we never got around to tackling much of my childhood background, on very short acquaintance he was able to see a creative side. "Have you ever thought of getting a camera?"

Taking a cue from one of my most favored cinematographers, Satyajit Ray, I spent a year snapping anything that caught my eye. The smallest aspects of the natural world drew my attention. Throughout this period, although my husband offered encouragement, I felt I needed sufficient independence from him to voice my true feelings about the asymmetry I had begun feeling at home. At the same time, no matter how estranged I had become from my mother, I wanted to be able to send her a small supplement to help ease her declining years. I had no income yet to call my own, and although we had a joint bank account, when I raised the prospect of opening an account of my own, to my immense surprise my husband voiced reluctance. The notion of the new economists that women's work should register as part of the GNP, still then an alarming idea, bolstered my own demand. I persisted and at last he agreed. The sense that I had my own resources, however limited, made me feel as though I could talk to my therapist in somewhat greater candor. And buy film for my Nikon.

Within a year I had exchanged it for a basic Super 8, which I took to an anti–Vietnam War demonstration for its maiden voyage, filming the thousands upon thousands of people flooding down San Francisco's Market Street in one single take, first at 24 frames per second; then 16, finally swooping in at 12, focusing the last frames into a red tulip in the hands of a demonstrator, aiming straight into its black heart.

I was beginning to give myself room to forge a new identity, this one shaped by work. But still riddled with a sense of self-doubt and a need to hedge my bets, my way back to a life in the theater would require yet another detour. I enrolled in the film department at San Francisco State University, trying to balance film theory with a practicum. The practicum won out, with students grouping themselves into technicians, directors, and actors. Quite naturally I fell in with the latter group. But after one semester, I became convinced that transferring a cinematic vision onto film stock would never be my forte. The results struck me as crude at best and wide of the mark, the effort far outweighing any satisfactory outcome. More to the point, I sensed that raising the astronomical sums needed to complete any in-depth project would always bar me from serious work in film. But at semester's end, if nothing else, film study gave me an objective look at the quality of my own performance. Why not admit it: it was the theater I loved. At last I surrendered to its invitation.

Enrollment in the drama department at San Francisco State had yet to meet computer technology. The registration lines spilled out way past the quad; in tents and deck chairs, thousands of students camped overnight holding their spots in the reg line, swallowing the inconvenience and at the same time benefiting from those face-to-face encounters, which advanced social bonds while yielding useful information about which classes promised the best rewards. Every drama student I talked to down the line mentioned one name in particular, Paul Rebillot, but after hours of waiting, when I reached the head of the line, his classes were already full. I had to find alternatives, but I paid Rebillot a visit.

Slight of build, with a shock of sandy blonde hair combed to the side and a persuasive way about him, he assured me that, although his overflowing enrollments were the source of some embarrassment given that his colleagues—some of them at least—were unable to fill their own classes, he would find a way to include me the following semester. At the time, I had no way of knowing he'd become my theater mentor.

That first semester, I managed to grasp the essentials of what direction for the stage must be about, namely deriving every single aspect of the mise-en-scène from one centralizing image. This attention to structure came to shape my theater and my later work as a writer. Meantime, I learned by doing, portraying characters in scenes by Genet and Brecht among many others and directing Pinter's *The Dumbwaiter* (where, with the collaboration of student actors, I was able to experiment with heightening tension) and Beckett's *Act without Words II* (where I discovered through control of pacing how to direct for humor in a text that made provision for it only by indirection). I directed my actors to trust the perceptions of their audience by *never referring to what they were doing*, and in so doing I learned that by trusting an audience's intelligence, I could direct in terms of understatement. This notion would become the principle underlying the sparse nature of my writing.

The following semester I began to work with the man who became my mentor. As a director, Rebillot's genius was to find the visual and psychic energy that brought the text to a life so immediate and startling, it left an audience stunned. His ability to transport a public to another world centered around his choice of performance material favoring themes relating to his own deeply held ideas about power and responsibility, illusion and reality, and matters of the unexplained. His skill working with actors by triggering their imaginations allowed them to find within themselves how to place any direction within their grasp. From his scene study section I learned the fine balance that comes from exploiting character contradiction.

That semester he was directing a production of Euripides' *Bacchae*. Although I sat in, observing daytime rehearsals, I felt constrained from joining the cast because the nighttime schedule conflicted with my responsibilities at home. I would continue to feel this conflict for some time, no matter how compelling I found any of my theatrical commitments, but in working with Rebillot, I determined to follow a course of studies that allowed me to acquire a skill. If I anticipated any goal, it would be one outside any rigid academic framework, but it would become the skill set that would determine the nature of my path.

My goal rather was to question received notions of what audiences routinely expected of theater. I wanted to evoke the kind of performance behavior that would challenge it and implicate it in unsettling ways and to reveal what a deeply authentic exchange between performers might feel like. Even before reading Artaud and Grotowski, my ideas had become solidified. I was reaching for the archetype, that place where the dailiness of living is shed and the door opens to the deep time underpinning life itself.

Thanks to a group of fellow students willing to experiment, the opportunity came my way to investigate kinetic sources of light and shadow using both natural and mechanical objects. We set to work in the undefined space of a rehearsal hall. Taking as a springboard the moon's blood-hungry soliloquy from García Lorca's *Blood Wedding*, we developed a tone poem of words, sounds, and movement.

Our materials consisted of stripped tree branches, a naked lightbulb mounted on a movable tripod, and for our reflector, a handheld repurposed aluminum pot lid some fourteen inches in diameter. The actors manipulated the branches throwing wind-whipped shadows on the bare walls. Two of them used the interplay between the single light source and the reflector to cast a moonlike shimmer through the silhouette of what appeared to be a forest come alive. Such a barebones description conveys only the sketchiest sense of this, the first of my experimental stagings, but this mise-en-scène became a formative kernel for the work that was to evolve over the next twelve years.

Punctuated by some of the stunning noh and kabuki stage conventions derived from his service stint in occupied Japan, Rebillot's direction of *Bacchae* turned out to be a spectacular triumph. Its concluding image, that of the god Dionysus mounted on a high revolving platform, every inch of his body anointed in gold, turned out to be a gesture of such mockery, it bore the shock value of blasphemy. It left its audience stunned, unable to move or clap or rise up from their seats.

At the same time Rebillot was directing *Bacchae*, he came up for tenure. The vote went against him. In response, and perhaps further galvanized by the resistance taking place from Paris to Berkeley and all over the student world, we drama students went out on strike as a body, a harbinger of the campus-wide strike that would occur a year later. Shortly thereafter, Stanford offered Rebillot a tenure-track position, but a nearly fatal car accident left him benched for the remainder of the year.

A substitute was hired to replace him. From the first, his approach distressed me, especially his habit of picking on and haranguing young women students. One incident stood out: he badgered a young woman student who must have felt particularly vulnerable that day till he'd reduced her to tears. None of my classmates seemed inclined to object. A half-generation older than most of them, I felt obliged to make a point of walking out. I shut the door behind me.

In the absence of appropriate instruction, I began initiating improvisatory sessions with some of my fellow students. In the atmosphere of growing tension just before the 1969–1970 student strike, our unscheduled workshops led to a question I felt needed to be addressed: *Was there ever a time when it became right for an artist not to continue speaking?* It is a question that has stayed with me throughout my writing life, expressing itself—with finality—in *Redoubt* (Wings Press, 2004).

> The desert is gone. I have no memory of the dunes, of how they sighed or groaned or turned over in their sleep. Or how, grain by grain, they ground up time into infinitesimal particles. Here, when they talk of it, they say the valley yields the ripest, reddest fruits. So we are blessed. . . .
>
> Sometimes, when night falls early—here in the valley—before the door closes—you can hear someone, immured somewhere, in another room—someone—a girl, or a woman perhaps—wailing softly, as if someone were choking back sobs. But there is no room, of course. And no sign of any woman.
>
> Sometimes I imagine—I let myself imagine—that it is me in there. I imagine that the sound might be coming from inside my throat.

My question was one that would eventually lead to my silence as a writer of fiction and my embrace of nonfiction. My 2009 project covering Jean Blum and her work with immigrant detention marks that turning point.

8. Strike

It was at the height of the Vietnam War that Ronnie Davis produced a Radical Theater Festival in fall 1968 at San Francisco State. The Mime Troupe performed *L'Amant Militaire*, a commedia piece by Goldoni that toured campuses throughout the United States. The Bread and Puppet Theater, directed by Peter Schumann, performed "A Man Says Good-Bye to His Mother" and "King Story" with a handful of performers (Schumann himself was one of them) and a number of puppets and set pieces. Produced as street theater designed to tell a story and staged around minimal text, freeze-frame gestures illustrated each line, the occasional dissonance between words and visual stage life providing humor, irony, and at times deep pathos. "King Story" offered the image of a fear-driven society whose paranoia eventually leads to a total loss of freedom. The concluding tableau offered a Godzilla-like image, monstrous and terrifying, accompanied by the eerily prescient final line, "Then Death came," followed by utter silence. In the quiet, audiences heard the distant voices of children playing in the park, of mothers' voices calling to them. It was a silence in which life and death encountered one another.

Far removed from "official" theater practice, what distinguished Schumann's prophetic artistic, political, and collective vision put him at the forefront of twentieth-century theater-making, not just in the United States but throughout the world. I had never seen a performance pack such power in such a very small containment. From him I took the simple mise-en-scène techniques which stood us in good stead when, two months later, almost the entire San Francisco State student body walked out in what turned out to be the longest-lasting student strike in U.S. history.

Its catalyzing issue was twofold: students wanted a black studies department, something the trustees strongly disfavored, and in a secret memo apparently leaked by student whistleblowers, the trustees planned to put an end to the Experimental College, a branch of State that worked directly in the Bay Area community, promoting student participation in various external projects aimed at social change.

Teams of strikers, myself included, disrupted those classes still in session, urging students to get out and join the strike. San Francisco State's notorious president, S. I. Hayakawa, called in the San Francisco tactical squad. That day hundreds of protesting students swarmed the quad, me among them, shouting our demands at top pitch. To get a better view I backed away from the crowd toward the perimeter—and barely escaped the cordon of tac squad lining up behind me.

More than four hundred students were arrested. The paddy wagon dashboards had been pre-equipped with stones, bricks, and other projectiles, all carefully numbered, to be slapped into the hands of arrestees as they were booked. One of my colleagues—who happened to be black—was deliberately beaten and bloodied before being pinned with an attempted murder charge. The drama faculty's reaction was swift: any students benefiting from financial aid found their funds cut off. Male students joining the strike were threatened with withdrawal of their draft deferment status. That day gave me a firsthand experience of massive police brutality. It was a day I'd never forget.

Day Six

The manipulation of language to serve unconstitutional ends is reflected in the directives of the office of Detention and Removal, a subagency of ICE, which calls its ten-year plan "Endgame," an eerie echo of the "Final Solution," the term preferred by the Nazi Third Reich referring to extermination. Its goal was to "remove" all removable aliens by 2012, including 590,000 persons ignoring deportation orders, and 630,000 "criminal" aliens (most of them charged with minor offenses such as broken taillights and entry without inspection), a total of 1.2 million souls. And, according to Marjorie Meyers, chief federal defender of south Texas, people convicted of illegal reentry were actually receiving anywhere from four to eight years in jail.

In a 2008 conference call to investors from company headquarters in Tennessee, CoreCivic's CEO got specific about inmate "care": "The intent now is to detain everyone that's apprehended at the border and charge them initially with something called 'entry without inspection.' That will be a misdemeanor, requiring somewhere between 15 and 30 days of detention.... Persons with [a] deportation [order] or minimum conviction, which means someone who ... committed [a] misdemeanor, will face a felony charge, which could lead to six months to two years of detention or incarceration." Enthused by the administration's fiscal 2009 budget, he stated, "We see that the budget supports a detention population of 33,000 inmate detainee beds—that's up from 27,500 the previous year and quite above what the ... original budget was. What I am most encouraged about is everything we are hearing says 33,000 is still not enough." And the Trump administration is asking for 46,000 beds, many assigned to babies, unaccompanied minors, and children in detention and separated from their parents, many of whom have been deported.

Reacting to ICE's "Operation Return to Sender," which increased its fugitive teams' 2003 arrest quota from 125 to 1,000 a day, the ACLU's Jenni Gainsborough stated the obvious: "[There is] a basic philosophical problem when you begin turning over the administration of prisons to people who have a [vested] interest in keeping people locked up."

Together with a group of drama students, I turned playwright for our agitprop (agitation/propaganda) group, touring other nearby state campuses, aiming to shut them down in sympathetic strikes. The simple expository techniques borrowed from Peter Schumann became an effective mode of expression, and after graduation it became a form I would bring with me when I accepted a job as drama director at Paltenghi, a black youth recreation center in San Francisco's Haight neighborhood. Creating their own masks of Celastic, and developing a freeze-frame mime show, *The Slave Ship*, its text based on the Middle Passage, the Paltenghi drama group made Schumann's form their own. That summer they went on to perform their piece to warm acclaim in one of San Francisco's parks. They formally adopted me. "You our mother," they assured me, a gesture I found deeply touching.

During the six-month duration of the strike, I commuted between Stanford and San Francisco State—a distance of some thirty-five miles—participating actively as a bootlegger in Rebillot's acting classes and his spring semester production of *The Cuchulain Cycle*, four Yeats plays. During its development we began to forge a peer relationship that took on the complexion of an apprenticeship, one characterized by mutual respect and an easy sense of give and take. He invited me to probe with him Yeats' symbolically embedded meanings—in established theaters, a task normally assigned to a dramaturg—exploiting their hidden signs for the basic shapes that would determine directorial design. Because such relationships traditionally presuppose reciprocation, every week I prepared dinner for his Palo Alto commune on our three rehearsal nights.

I hoped that my participation might allow observation of some of the many other directorial elements from which Rebillot would draw, notably actor development. However, that was not to be. Early on he appointed me leader of the chorus, a role requiring rehearsal away from the main stage, preventing me from attending the scene rehearsals that might have furthered my own skills. Left to my own devices, I had to learn by doing, and I drew on what I had observed of the previous year's *Bacchae* rehearsals: how to pitch a chorus and how to find the rhythmic dynamism of the text. Some nights rehearsals kept me away from home till after midnight. We had found a surrogate mother (better equipped than I) to care for the children after school and involve them in creative projects till Felix ended his hospital day and took them home to supper.

Artistic temperaments are rarely in tune with academia, and Rebillot was no exception. His personal style was too freewheeling for the moss-backed culture of The Farm. In the midst of *Cuchulain* rehearsals, in a kind of déjà vu, Stanford terminated him. But both *Bacchae* and the *Cuchulain Cycle* a year apart, were the gifts of a true master at his peak. Sadly, never again was he to enjoy the kind of institutional support that would allow him to continue his work as the extraordinary theater-maker that he was. Worse still, it was a loss that went ignored and unlamented. Although he was eventually able to reinvent himself as a human potential movement guru, his demise as a theater-maker represents a significant loss to the cultural life of the Bay Area and to the country at large.

In the tense atmosphere at San Francisco State, the strike had come to a head. Like many other top faculty, theater director Dugald MacArthur was quick to book flights to other universities in search of another posting. It would be his final semester and my last opportunity to work with him. Under his direction I took the leading role as Charlotte Corday in his epic staging of *Marat/Sade*, a benefit both in terms of further honing my own directorial strengths and developing my ability to elicit deep actor response. From him I learned something of the art of gesture and in-depth character development. But soon it became clear to me that, without a faculty member left to direct my final project, if a degree were to be awarded me at all, I'd have to sit for the exit exam. Reluctantly I did.

Because of massive student insistence, once the strike was settled, San Francisco State became the first U.S. university to include a black studies program, opening the way for ethnic studies and Chicano studies programs nationwide. I was back attending class, about to graduate, and in rehearsal for three separate scene studies (fig. 5) under student directors when one evening, returning home late from attending project finals, I found an ambulance parked in the street outside. As I gave way to panic, I heard my voice rising. "Is that my husband you have in there?" Citing privacy concerns, the attendant refused to answer. I grew even more alarmed. Then I saw with my own eyes. It was Felix. He'd been brought home in a state of collapse. Ever since our Charleston days, when it first made its appearance, his

FIG. 5. Cecile Pineda appearing in a student production of Brecht's *Jewish Wife*. (Courtesy of James Oren.)

vertigo had progressively worsened. At times, when he was unable to stand, I would have to fetch him home from the office. "He always seems to get sick when you're having finals," a Mime Troupe colleague observed. Her remark gave me pause. But now, even though I had come to that terrifying postgraduate jumping-off country known as WHAT'S NEXT, whatever happened, I knew there could be no turning back. I recognized that by temperament I was not a theorist. In one form or another, I would have to make art, and although in the making there might be teaching moments, the stage, not the classroom, was going to be my venue.

With the departure of Dugald MacArthur, in the absence of a thesis chair, I came to think there was no reason I couldn't mount an independent project in the larger community on my own. But without institutional affiliation, such an endeavor had to involve not only directing but producing as well. The Bay Area had not yet fallen victim to vulture developers and shark-landlordism. Church sanctuaries still could be had as performance venues for a hundred dollars a night, and their architecture could provide that *set accompli* required for a production of T. S. Eliot's *Murder in the Cathedral*, and at no additional expense. Ever since my own hard-won college tour, Eliot's text had been simmering on my back burner. The challenge now was to transform the tidy little pageant suggested by Eliot's measured words into a riveting theatrical event. I pondered what production values I might lend it to resonate with the popular resistance (in which I continued to participate) against the Vietnam War. And how its mise-en-scène might reflect Rebillot's own debacle at Stanford. But without a shred of backing, where would I find the resources to bring off what seemed like a major project? Would I be able to line up venues? How would I go about recruiting actors, designers, composers, and technicians? Or raise a budget sufficient to rent rehearsal and performance space, pay actors and collaborators, and provide costumes, props, and sets?

How did women artists in conventional middle-class marriages run households, raise children? How did they manage without the help of servants? The answer was they didn't. Certainly not very well. For the past two years I had been raising a family while scrambling to take classes, attend directorial workshops and rehearsals, rehearse scenes, play major roles. But what was the point of all that effort if now that the moment was upon me, I felt unequal to the task? There were days the enormity of such a prospect loomed terrifying. My old feelings of anxiety returned. The challenge before me felt too much like a quantum leap. Some days I stopped myself from thinking about it altogether, but no matter how much I tried to squelch it, the more my terror grew. Yet when I finally appealed to Felix, he voiced no objection. On the contrary, I found him encouraging and generous of spirit. My bluff had been called—if it had been a bluff in the first place—and now I could claim no more excuses to hide behind, freedom terrified me even more.

At last the idea came to me to carve out some kind of space between, a place to deal with my insecurities and my feelings of self-doubt, somewhere to find perspective. On the summit of Marin County's Mount Tamalpais, I would spend the day in contemplation. I would stay as long as it took to know what it was I had to do. I headed out of San Francisco, north across the Golden Gate into Mill Valley, past Ash Street where as a family we settled when we first came to California some eight years before, and where the road begins climbing, following its many twists and turns till at last it levels out at the grove where as a young family we used to come picnicking and where in the declining light of the afternoon our sons had great fun capturing blue-bellied lizards and letting them go free. In the spring the slope was wont to burst with color, but by early fall, the rains were long past, the tall grasses burned out. I spread my blanket under a stand of oaks. My gaze swept the far distance to the south. Above the clouds, the San Francisco skyline etched the far horizon in relief; below, a solid bank of fog blocked out all but the sound of surf.

It was near the same high meadow where Rebillot had held his workshop the previous summer—the place where I'd first voiced the idea that would lead to my work with him at Stanford. What about that apprenticeship? Had it given me the confidence my project would require? Almost at once, my mind rebelled. A thousand fears began their demon clamoring. *One, two, three, four, we don't want your fucking war.* That time marching up Hayes Hill. Balloons, baby carriages, the hot sun: *Ho, Ho, Ho Chi Minh! Ho Chi Minh is gonna win!* Running the Super 8 that time: long shot, medium, straight into the tulip's heart. Black out. That time with the ambulance. *Who's in there? I think my husband's in there.* Carrying him on my back that time. *Always sick when you're away from home.*

Too many voices pushed their way in. I lost track of why I'd come. The hours passed. The sun's slant rays shot the hills with gold. Quite suddenly, a tall young man appeared, blond, ponytailed, in his hands a bamboo flute. He bowed to me with "May I play for you?" I patted a corner of blanket, where I invited him to sit. He began to play. Threads scattered on the wind, thin at first, the notes gathered sweep, weaving arabesques in the quickening air, curling back to silence. He rose, bowed, and left without a word.

I had been visited. For the next two hours I ran through the long accounting of all the seemingly unrelated things life had tossed my way—double-entry bookkeeping; raising funds; managing an office; running a business for a year; learning how to think about mise-en-scène, what a light design could do, and how to pitch a chorus, how to recruit actors, how to secure venues.

I had no excuses: I knew all these things. I knew I knew them. And above all, knowing them felt good. A sense of calm came over me, a sense of confidence newfound. And the money? If nothing else, the budget would come from my work at the youth center. And I still had my mother's Thessalonians to puff up my sails. The sun began to set. At last I was ready to take the quantum leap that would catapult me into public life.

9. Theatre of Man

Theatre of Man was the turning point, the threshold where I would leave housewifery behind and assume my own distinct identity. It was the point where in earlier generations, women might have returned home, however discontent, to resume the subservient existence of the good chatelaine. But I was born on the cusp of a new way of living, passing through that brief respite in U.S. history where as a society, we felt the excitement of what might be possible. We exchanged eye contact with strangers. Perfect strangers hailed each other in the streets. We would start a feminist movement, topple a presidency, and end a war. And although we were never lucky enough to know the comforts of a government such as Chile enjoyed before the CIA-fomented coup of September 11, 1973, the sixties were as close as we would ever come to knowing a national happiness—at least within my lifetime.

It was a transitional time in American theater as well, a time that reflected in its energy and inventiveness that same catalyzing spirit, that of the sixties and early seventies. My own first years of theater-making led from the derivative work spawned by my apprenticeship toward collective creation. But with no organizational net to catch me, no funding other than what I might be able to raise myself—at first all of it from salaried work—no publicity or promotional apparatus, no way of announcing auditions except through classified advertising, and no real venue to hold auditions, it seemed like a fool's leap. Yet the alternative was out of the question.

An early mission statement reads: "Theatre of Man expresses through its work a new consciousness of the need for community, welding together forms of sacred theater and concerns of a theater which help us make sense emotionally and intellectually of the world around and inside us. Using techniques of experimental theatre, the ensemble creates a total theatrical experience in which sound, music, movement, and dance are combined to create kaleidoscopic dreams, visions, and mysteries."

First auditions, held in the sanctuary of San Francisco's Glide Memorial Church, drew more than one hundred actors. Tightly structured sound and movement exercises, designed to reveal how well people responded to working together and how available they were to their own bodies, allowed me to pare the contenders down to manageable numbers. Later, in a two-person improvisation, one actor drew a knife on his partner. I called a freeze. He dropped the knife. I waved him off the stage with a "thank you very much." I had met my first dangerous challenge, but as an early warning, it was an event that would stand me in good stead.

Gradually I found my footing. After a week of trials I had a working company of twenty, a good many of them highly skilled, a few barely experienced. I even congratulated myself that their lack of training was all to the good and that, as a director, I would have no need to cut through any acquired mannerisms I found inauthentic. On tour at the time, the San Francisco Mime Troupe offered us the use of its rehearsal loft—albeit a refrigerated one—to begin our work. I had a script, one with which the intervening years had made me more than familiar, and I had a rehearsal formula. The evenings included warmup exercises and deep relaxation, followed by a kind of spiraling sequence of exercises leading to increasingly complex improvisations, and ended with discussion before the company adjourned for the night. We had ten weeks.

The prospect of drawing on the devices of the Greek theater, such as stichomythia, to heighten tension, turning Eliot's well-behaved

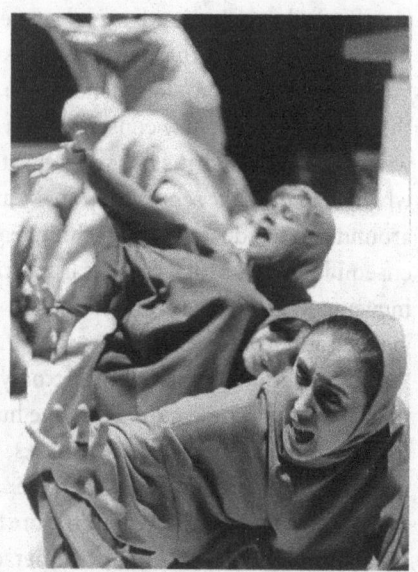

FIG. 6. "For the chorus, I had nine women." (*top to bottom*) Kathy Ennis, Leslie Robertson, and Susan Jess in *Murder in the Cathedral* performed at Grace Cathedral, San Francisco, by Theatre of Man in 1969–1970. (Courtesy Howard Harawitz.)

words into a stunning theatrical event, excited me. But we had no name, and for publicity and promotional purposes, we would need one. Inspired by Joyce's "What is that word known to all men?" as a name, *Theatre of Man* fell short of what I envisioned; for one thing, it left out more than half the human race, but at the time I found no better words for what I had in mind.

Rehearsals took off in a burst of energy. Borrowing liberally from Rebillot's directorial vocabulary, I assigned applicable passages for the actors to develop choreographically. For the chorus I had nine women (fig. 6). At first I broke them up into teams of three, each improvising on the same passage, choreographing the figures and gestures that lent physicality to each given image. It was this work with the chorus that I found most engaging. Two actors portrayed two aspects of Thomas, one the public Archbishop of Canterbury in all the austerity of his high office; the other, the loincloth-clad figure of his self-narrative as the martyred Christ.

We still lacked a lighting design and crew. One evening, a group of folks appeared in the loft, cowboy boots, patchouli oil, leather fringe jackets, and the occasional ear stud, emblems all of the counterculture. "We heard you got your shit together," they announced. "We're here to do your lights." How they found us remains a mystery to this day. If I care to, I can imagine my flute-playing good angel directed them to us. They joined the production team along with designer Gerd Mairandres, a schoolmate from the drama department (later of the San Francisco Opera) and Bill Young, our composer in residence, recruited from the San Francisco State music department. In my initial discussions with him I described how I envisioned a musical component punctuating the text at heightened moments and how it might stand in for curtains or customary blackouts unavailable in church settings. "Does it sound like this?" He sat at the piano, improvising around Benjamin Britten's *War Requiem*. War was certainly on our minds. We were some fourteen years into America's debacle in Vietnam, with six more years to go.

As a production team, I felt we were complete, all but for one missing piece. I was working without a graduate thesis director. Rebillot, still living in the area, accepted an honorarium to serve as my advisor. Ten days before we opened, he joined us in the loft. His three generous pages of notes emphasized his main concern: rhythmic dynamics. As a model on which to plot them, he suggested the biorhythms of animal behavior, interludes of feeding, hunting, fleeing, copulation, and rest. In them we would find the pulse.

I managed to book a three-month run that took us traveling to a dozen sanctuaries all over the Bay Area, from Belvedere to Berkeley, Hayward to San Mateo, issuing promotion in the form of posters and flyers, publicity in the form of press releases, and scoring a few advance pieces which ran in the mainstream press. By our ten-week deadline we were ready. We opened in San Francisco's Glide Memorial sanctuary. Every seat was taken. Huge projections of William Blake's images, his fiery falling angel among them, substituted for curtains. Besides my husband, in attendance opening night were my therapist and Paul Rebillot, accompanied by all the members of his commune. And in a stunning coincidence, Dugald MacArthur, freshly resigned from San Francisco State that summer to accept the drama chairmanship at Temple University, happened to be passing in the darkened street outside. Drawn by our strange harmonies, he came just in time to scoop up one of the last remaining tickets.

The performance came to a close. Unseen in the narthex, I joined the women of the chorus to build the closing aleatoric sound cloud. We let our voices crest, at last returning them to silence. The audience sat stunned, unable to stir. Some mysterious transformation had come over them; they were not sure what. At last, they managed to clap and rise from their seats.

We had survived our opening night. The evening left me exhausted and so jazzed I gave myself no time to breathe. Above all else, if I was going to give the company notes before the following night's performance, I wanted to make sure to get Rebillot's feedback. He received me in his kitchen. We sat on utility stools. After some hesitation, he pronounced his verdict. The production was put together flawlessly, not a note was missing, but in the end it left him cold. It was a mechanical, dead thing. Crushed, I returned home, barely able to blurt out his remarks. "Oh, no, no, no, no. That's not what I saw," Felix objected. "I could see him sitting one row to the front of me. He kept gasping, completely awed by what he saw."

It seemed inconceivable to me that my mentor might have withheld something so vital to me. Inconceivable after our close collaboration. Something struck me as seriously out of joint. That week I kept my regular appointment with my therapist. "I had to see if your expectations of yourself were realistic," he told me. "I found they were." Yet no matter how reassuring, the words of a psychiatrist could never compensate for the verdict of someone I held in such high regard, someone to whom, throughout our long collaboration, I had related as apprentice to master.

Midway through our run, as the eight-hundredth anniversary of Thomas Becket's martyrdom drew near, San Francisco's Grace Cathedral invited Theatre of Man to perform. Much as we felt honored, we soon discovered that there was no way to transpose our work, such as it was, into a venue of such massive scale, with a six-second-long reverberation, without simplifying and enlarging the choreographic movement and abridging the text to accommodate the much slower delivery dictated by the cathedral's sound delay. We had two days to rehearse.

We opened on the solstice. The seats were packed. Despite the small mishaps one might have expected, against the imposing Gothic scale of the architectural background, the performance took on an awesome cast. Back in the narthex, the nine women of the chorus yielded the last note of our sound cloud to the silence of the cathedral. The audience sat stunned. At last they remembered to clap, and we handed each one a lighted candle as they went out into the cold December night.

A stranger approached me. "How did you do that?" he wanted to know. At the moment I was at a loss to say. There was no question that my apprenticeship had equipped me with a sense of how a space might be endowed with some kind of mysterious visual power and some cognizance of what effect the rhythm of words might evoke. In his own work, Rebillot often drew from the Tarot's higher arcana to derive visual and symbolic inspiration. If nothing else, I had used the minor suits to emblemize Eliot's characters: swords for the knights, brass pentacles for the paten-bearing priests, cups full of liquid fire in which the tempters offered Becket their poisoned drink, and wands for the women who bore dead palm branches in their hands.

But for a director to be able to project a world to an audience, a particular theatrical language is called for. Whereas with fiction the writer alone needs to project that vision, the theater requires an entire company to work together as one mind. In particular, physical theater, Theatre of Man's idiom, relies on the specific language of sound and movement improvisations in which the actor engages in the sign language of full bodily expression. Negotiating such a language involves elaborating increasingly complex exercises to address the theme (or themes) central to a particular performance work.

It was after a performance in Grace Cathedral, from the far distance of the narthex, that I saw Felix walking toward me down the center aisle, accompanied by an unfamiliar woman, a woman whom he favored with a certain look. Even at that distance it was a gesture I understood. I had not been the recipient of such a look for a very long time.

The run ended in early spring. We struck the show for the last time, hefted the cement light trees, props, and costumes—all but the dead branches—up the two long flights of stairs—twenty-four of them—and into the basement of the Noe Valley house my family shared. All actors received their weekly pay from equally shared box office receipts. We had no grants as yet to sustain us—after all, this was only a graduate thesis project. We took a few days off, scheduling an evaluation for the following week.

Meantime I had two appointments to keep. One was a visit I had planned from the time Felix alerted me to Rebillot's reaction. Although I failed to realize it at first, it would mark the close of my apprenticeship. Once again, Rebillot received me in his kitchen. I broke the silence. "How could you do that to me? That show was full of feeling. It was full of love." I waited for his answer. When it came, his response shocked me—and saddened me too. "Don't you think it may have had something to do with the state of my own work at the time?" was what he said. Was it an apology? Never stated. An evasion? Not explicitly. It did not escape me that it fell short of any other acknowledgment. But whatever it was not, I perceived it as a recognition of his own sense of responsibility.

Our visit was at an end. I stumbled down the porch stairs of the elegant Pacific Heights mansion he shared with the members of his commune. I remembered my feeling that time seeing my father, old and stooped in the distance, and accepting our estrangement. On the few subsequent occasions when we found ourselves together, Rebillot always referred to me as his student, never as a colleague.

With time, I have come to recognize how two of the essential leave-takings of my life—from him and from my father—bear a certain resemblance, and how in the difference lie many years of coming to better terms with myself. Both were mentors, one my father, the other my artistic master; I felt a complex and ambivalent love for each. Although I chose the moment to leave them, both leave-takings occurred under a cloud, one stormy, one much more nuanced, the difference, say, between a conflagration and quite natural decay. But it seems to me the big difference is that there was no opportunity to confront my father. We had never negotiated any agreement that permitted a demand for fairness from him, whereas Paul allowed space for that moment—and I demanded it. My father could not live a life in which he could express his sexual preference openly, whereas Rebillot could, and perhaps for that reason, our leave-taking, if not more generous, was certainly more respectful. My father, not granting himself the right to his own sexuality, had tried to punish me for mine.

While I shared with Felix the details of my leave-taking from the master under whom I'd served an extraordinary apprenticeship, I made no mention of what I had seen far down the aisle of Grace Cathedral on that cold December night. I had forgotten all about it. I was entering a five-year period of denial, utter and complete.

My other visit was to my therapist. Consciously I felt I no longer needed his help. I discharged myself from his care. Probably I believed I had come to a place where I knew what it was I loved. I didn't feel it necessary to tell him that quite recently a member of my company had urged me to pay attention to my health, a warning I ignored out of hand. It never occurred to me that the health he might have had in mind was something other than physical. And unconsciously it may well have been because I was entering a period where for the next five years I would choose to live a lie. Events would show how prematurely I'd acted dismissing him.

I imagined I was still fulfilling the final requirements of a master's thesis by scheduling a project evaluation. The company held what I thought would be our last meeting. I was unprepared for what followed. Twenty people gazed at me expectantly. What's next? they wanted to know. They waited silently for what I had to say. I sat facing them, dumbfounded. The stress involved producing and directing *Murder in the Cathedral*, followed by our three-month performance season, had engaged me so intensely it hadn't yet occurred to me that a time would ever come when I could see beyond the immediate pressures of the moment.

I had drawn together a company! An exceptionally talented company! They looked to me, their trust testimony to the quality of our work. But I had given the future no thought. Now it suddenly came to me there was every good reason to keep them together. But how? With what? I had no arrows in my quiver.

Inspired perhaps by the rhythmic interludes we'd used to project Blake's images, Bill Young, our composer in residence, brought to my attention his engravings for the Book of Job. For anyone drawn to the art of the nineteenth-century English poet, this particular engraving cycle represents his recasting of the Tarot, in which he maps the story of Job's trial on a solar eclipse. An eclipse had certainly played an important role in my own childhood, but what I didn't know at the time is that up to that point, in one form or another, every theater company that tried to work with the Book of Job had met with disaster. But that spring of 1970, I was as hooked as I was baffled by the opacity of Blake's drawings. Even Blake experts occasionally stub their toes, but in Blake's work, even though I had done absolutely no preparatory work to address it, I thought I recognized the kind of challenge my foolhardiness wouldn't allow me to pass up.

From the beginning, I had had a clear vision of *Murder*. Its great success seems to me to have been rooted in my fully fleshed sense of the sound and look of it—some of it based on familiarity with the spirit of the Middle Ages, some of it based on long acquaintance with the text, and some inspired by use of the Tarot images. For its container, I had relied on the architectural setting, ready made, that any sanctuary I managed to book might provide. And with my composer collaborator, we developed the sound landscape to support it.

But producing a performance project meant having all the lead time to prepare, from early spring when the season ended to mid-September, when auditions had to be scheduled to draw a company together, a quiet and solitary time to gather my thoughts: What theme might we address? How might I relate it to what was happening in the world? What sources would we tap? And above all, what performance space might make itself available? And what might it look and sound like?

The Book of Job originates in an early non-Hebraic Middle Eastern culture—a desert culture—which suggests that water, and the thirst for water might determine the nature of the god it held dear. And indeed when Job's prayers are finally answered, the voice of his god comes to him in the form of a whirlwind. With Blake as our springboard, rehearsals began. When actors asked me for explanations, my response was, "That's what we're working to discover," a remark that put them off, and whereas they had come to know me as a director who seemed able to field almost any question during the period during which we had developed *Murder*, now I disappointed them with a barrage of mystification.

Quite predictably, they soon lost patience. And quite predictably, instead of letting them know that if they were disgruntled, they had every right to pick up and leave, I held on because the prospect of a work hiatus loomed as something more terrifying than I wanted to entertain—perhaps because unconsciously I feared returning home to face something I lacked courage to face. Their impatience exploded in full rebellion. Our last meeting together turned into a wrenching confrontation. I wanted to keep them together. Instead, I turned my anger inward. Strung out to a fever pitch, I vaguely recognized that I seemed not to be acting quite rationally. Paranoia overtook me: someone was trying to burn down my house. Felix canceled all his office appointments to stay at home with me. On one of those first days he suggested I accompany him on an errand that couldn't be postponed. As we drove through the San Francisco streets, perhaps because it was the time of full moon, we passed a number of people acting out scenes of their inner lives. After three such episodes, Felix very kindly reassured me that what we had observed was real, not tricks of my own troubled mind.

It was time to reconnect with my therapist, who prescribed massive doses of Stelazine, and because no other beds were available, he had me hospitalized at San Mateo County hospital, a former psychiatry ward of the San Mateo jail, where I was placed in what had once been a cell. The cell next to mine housed an autistic child who in the deepest time of night awoke with horrifying screams. To reassure me, until dawn broke an attendant came to stay with me. She sat by my bedside knitting. Her name was Ofelia. Renamed Irma, Portuguese word for *sister*, she became the model for the first transformational character in my fiction.

After four days, when I failed to come down, my therapist began to fear he might be out of his depth. Whereas before my breakdown, I had the feeling I could remember every event of every day of my life, now I lost that sense. Five days disappeared. But not altogether. My inner being had simply sloughed its shell, busy apparently forming a new one—one that took some five days or so to set. Still at San Mateo during that time, with the materials provided, I drew an image of Helios' fiery chariot, led by four horses whose coats ranged from white to black. Was the image a reference to Blake's eclipse—and mine? Who or what did those four horses represent? Were they my ancestors, the grandparents I had never known? I called my image "chariot of the sun." I drew another titled "fuschia fetus." As became clear to me later, it hinted at my future: red to purple with absorbed rage, a strange chick pecking at its shell, waiting to be born.

A week later, I was discharged to a day program, and within the week I returned home. But I felt somehow my mind had been short-circuited, unable to operate at full capacity—if indeed I remembered at all what full capacity may have felt like. During the following six months, in the humblest acts of living, my spirit had to learn to mend itself, stumbling first before it could regain its balance. In this, I was fortunate. I had the love and support of my small family and my children to take care of.

Sometimes people ask me what it felt like to take leave of my senses. It's as if, quite simply, you've been evicted from yourself. Your whole world falls away. All the tricks you've learned to get by are forgotten. There's nothing left to fall back on, no sense of who you might be or where you might have come from or what dues you may have paid. Nowhere is your country, no one is your kin. You're stranded in a place unknown, surrounded by a world of strangers, like the four-year-old I used to be, abandoned by a father who liked to disappear. You're lost in the crack between the bed and the wall, and afraid you'll never make it out, but when you do—if you do—you will have had the opportunity to discover just how fragile your existence really is. With the gyroscope of time setting things to rights, sometimes such events prove to be immense blessings, no matter how darkly their arrival may first have come disguised. An echo of my near-death at the age of ten and my reaction after the birth of my firstborn, as those other events had, this crisis gave me time, time between caring for my family, time to heal. Time to think, to take walks, to allow myself things I normally didn't allow myself to do. And time to read.

Quite by happenstance I stumbled on *The Serpent* by Jean-Claude van Itallie, a script based on the Book of Genesis. Originally developed in their rehearsal process by the Open Theater, a company engaged in a similar kind of physical work, *The Serpent* left three scenes open, interludes that needed to be mounted at a company's discretion, an opportunity to learn how to build a full-length piece—a windfall at this stage in my directorial development. It allowed me to move away from scripted material altogether. For one thing, paying royalties for rights to *Murder in the Cathedral* represented a sizable portion of our 1969–1970 budget. We could operate more economically by developing our own performance scores. And perhaps, too, *Murder*'s dead palm branches suggested the use of found objects and stripped down production costs.

Felix and I were both drawn to the idea of staging a work based on Genesis. We discussed the Talmudic view of existence as emblemized by the spiral. *Serpent* would be a piece staged in the round. The question was, was I ready? Was I prepared once more to expose myself to risk? Would my family remain intact? Would we all survive and thrive?

Making art while raising small children and sustaining a middle-class marriage is hardly a prescription for sanity, neither of the self nor of other family members, and the long history of women artists suggests there are plenty of risks. Historically, to make art women were forced to find adaptive and often marginal accommodations: They became nuns or they loved other women. Or, very simply, they went mad. The rare exceptions were artists born to wealth or those financially able through marriage or a liaison eventually to support themselves through their work—some under assumed men's names.

Often successful women writers in particular seem to have re-

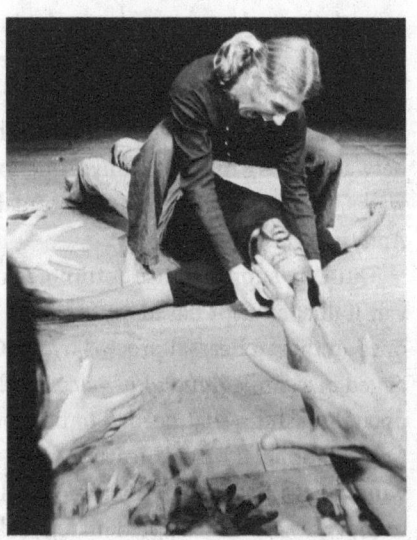

FIG. 7. "The work was impassioning." Harold Hector as Abel and Tom Shirley as Cain in Theatre of Man's 1971 production of *The Serpent*. (Courtesy of Ed Buryn.)

ceived far more than token attention from their fathers. I certainly fit that description; if there was anything else that made me exceptional, it was my drive to work and to create the conditions enabling me to work, no matter the risk—or the consequences. In the long view, I may have had my demon mother's Thessalonians to thank.

Six months later, I put out an audition call for *The Serpent*. I accepted nineteen actors, some of them much younger than me, one, a flower child, barely eighteen, a high school dropout with a taste for Walter Benjamin (Shelley Hirsch would go on to attract international recognition as an avant-garde composer-vocalist). In contrast to *Murder*, the production was decidedly stripped down, making use of rehearsal clothes and enamel canning kettles, but the work itself was impassioning (fig. 7). We came to identify one unscripted section ("I am a little man, I was not involved"), a section following a tableau of the Kennedy assassination, as "Shrimp Dance" because to develop it, we visited Steinhart Aquarium in Golden Gate Park, where as a company we observed thousands of brine shrimp gyrating in a frenzied ball of activity. But the fundamental building block on which our kind of physical theater practice depended always remained sound and movement exercises and, accompanying them, habituation by the actors to trust in the responding impulse. First thought, best thought, and, in our case, first impulse, best impulse. Implicit in that first impulse is the kind of truthfulness that comes when self-censoring is turned off.

The ultimate challenge was staging the "Begats," that litany of generation piled upon generation. To develop the soundscape, the company traveled to Lands End where, within the semidarkness of caves deep below the tide line, we listened to the surf pounding against the cliffs above. From that sound we derived a simple melody which became the score for the "Begats," a song of redemption derived from the great bed of the sea itself. We filled those enameled canners with water. They served as washbasins: pairs of actors bathed each other's faces and hands, humming the song born of the surf while intoning the names of generation upon generation to the constant drip of water. Fanning out beyond their own immediate circle, they invited audience members to join them.

The season came to a close. "The work ends with joy and hope," wrote one critic. "The last fifteen minutes of *The Serpent* shine with the washing away of sin and in a most extraordinary stroke, all those 'begats' you skipped over in your Bible are intoned with careful Hebraic pronunciation so that the legendary begins of Adam-Atman and Christ-Krishna leap to life again after many centuries of sleep." Surely a review to cherish, but Felix's comment struck me as more telling: "Your work shows a warmth I haven't seen before." Perhaps, after all, Rebillot had been right.

By 1972 we had begun to receive grants from the City of San Francisco Hotel Tax Fund, modest publicity help from the San Francisco Neighborhood Arts Association and corporations whose public relations offices I visited, attempting through trial and error to translate the nature of our work into some kind of stammering corporatese. We would no longer have to rely on our customary rotating series of rehearsal venues now that we could afford to rent a studio of our own in a repurposed San Francisco Howard Street warehouse better known as Project One (headquarters for the San Francisco Parking Enforcement in this postcultural age). But if we intended to build our audience, we needed to parlay the successes of *Murder* and *Serpent*.

FIG. 8. Stan Roth as Getrich Quicklips and John Rolling as the fox about to bamboozle another victim in *The Bear's Bash*, Theatre of Man's 1973 free show for kids in the San Francisco parks. (Courtesy of Victor Spigulis.)

What if we followed the Mime Troupe's example, offering free summer shows in the parks developed especially for children? If winter was meant for tragedy, why not provide the summer with a comedy?

Over the next three summers, I produced three free children's shows in the parks of San Francisco, among them *The Bear's Bash* (fig. 8), which in the absence of effective directorial control became something of a collective effort. We saw our reward in the wonderment and delight on the faces of children of all colors and social classes, all of them participating in the great democracy of laughter, triggered by our sly humor and visual shtick, much of it modeled on the style of the San Francisco Mime Troupe, whose star actress, Sandra Archer, I recruited to direct our first season, along with some of the troupe's most adept comedians, among them Joe Bellan and Darryl Henriques; and Steve Friedman, one of the troupe's resident playwrights, who scripted our first-season adaptation of the Russian folk tale *The Fool of the World and the Flying Ship*.

But with our scattershot experiment, we came shy of making any profits or building our winter audiences. We needed to keep to a single, clear artistic focus, one we would adhere to, to stick to work that probed those hidden aspects of the collective zeitgeist as they play themselves out in the realpolitik of the culture. Why, for example, despite the demonstrably more effective and life-sustaining approach of collaborative ways of living and working together, people seem to fall back on worlds characterized by competition, conflict, destruction, and murder; why people managed sooner or later to find themselves marching to the dictates of nightmare regimes; what assumptions underlie the sexual politics that shape how gender roles get parceled out.

I had never quite forgotten the degrading and manipulative maneuvers to which I'd had to resort during the time I rehearsed some of the male actors in the *Murder* company. Were sexual politics at the root of problems faced by women directors (still a rarity at that time)? For the next two years, in collaboration with playwright Doris Baizley, later of the Mark Taper Forum, I embarked on a project addressing gender role expectation, anticipating that somehow sexual politics as I had known them in the days of my pratfall employment were undergoing a positive change toward parity.

A performance description reads,

> *After Eurydice* uses the legend of Orpheus and Eurydice to explore the ways in which men and women experience one another, through the reality of the present, through memories, reflections, and dreams. The play is an odyssey through the consciousness and life of woman, through the labyrinthine masks which she is expected to assume [in] answer to the desires and fears of others, and which imprison woman and [man] alike. On [her] passage through the underworld, Eurydice visits the houses of hell where she relieves her childhood, womanhood, and old age. In the mirror of her visions, she perceives pieces of herself. [Her] journey is [the] struggle to reassemble those fragments of her identity.... [The work] uses masks, music, the word, and dance to distill new meaning from the old myth.

I chose the myth of Orpheus and Eurydice as emblematic of romantic love, and of the male pedestalization of the ideal woman (fig. 9). Our work that season was the culmination of an anthropological, sociological, and political workshop process.

Early in rehearsal, the war came home in the person of a recently

FIG. 9. Dan Fuller as the blindfolded Orpheus clasps the dead Eurydice, Esther Rivlin in *After Eurydice*, Theatre of Man's 1973 production. (Courtesy of John Clayton.)

discharged Vietnam vet. Fresh from the killing ground, he asked to be allowed to join our company as a way of reentering the normal world. Although rehearsals were already under way, I had no hesitation, but before making a commitment, I knew I needed to get a feeling from the company of the degree to which they would not only welcome but lend support to a late arrival, an arrival who had been to hell and needed to come back. The feeling was unanimous: we must help him reenter a world at peace, where the streets remained unbloodied, and where people came and went without the threat of death. No matter that throughout our run he needed to be reminded when his cues came up, we were there for him, a microsociety, helping him reacclimatize to the routines of daily living. By the end of our season, he'd found a job and a place to live, and he'd formed a significant relationship.

The cast of what came to be titled *After Eurydice* (meaning "according to Eurydice," or conversely, the collapse of the myth of the idealized woman) included an equal number of men and women, with composer in residence Bill Young collaborating, using original musical instruments built by Richard Waters. During our two intense years of development, at one point so deep was the schism between the genders that tension and distrust brought the work to a paralyzing halt. There was nothing for it but to declare a hiatus. We resumed work the following season. By then a new group of actors had coalesced, some from the old company, many recruited from a more recent audition.

In retrospect, the rehearsal process through which we developed the final performance score may well have been even more compelling than the actual performance. It was certainly more uncompromising. Of thirteen linked rituals, among them "Department Store," where women's gender images were parceled out, the most telling was titled "Men's World," which plotted the space in four quadrants in which "working," "eating and drinking," "dancing," and "sleep" were set up in a kind of baseball diamond. In the original improvisation the men's team was directed to create a world of equal role parity for women, a fact that does nothing to soften the message: that year the only roles assigned women by the men in our company turned out to be either overtly copulatory or procreative. In the original improvisation, the gay women of the company actually rebelled and ended the exercise.

Finding its resolution posed one of *Eurydice*'s most challenging problems. One of the guiding principles I had taken from my apprenticeship with Rebillot was the understanding that leading an audience through darkness required bringing it back into light. Would we leave matters unresolved as our explorations seemed to have concluded or would we invite the possibility of transformation?

We settled on a final scene. Three women, the virgin, the woman, and the crone, slapped Orpheus' nude body with palm prints of blood, emblemizing the rebirthing of men, all the while chanting a litany urging kindness and compassion and ending with a demand for recognition. It proposed a transformation rooted in forgiveness, ending with the lines: "We have journeyed long. This is my face." It was a transformation deeply personal to me (in my own role as the crone), though how it would play itself out in my own life had not yet become obvious. But our work during the 1971–1973 developmental period seemed to indicate that, far from improving, widely held views of gender roles hadn't changed that much. In the words of Erich Neumann, writing in 1955 in *The Great Mother*, the effect of power differentials between the sexes are fundamentally irreconcilable until such time as deeply held mythologies are brought into consciousness. And even then...

Still married at the time, I took my commitment seriously. At season's close, when a member of my company made romantic overtures, I decided to put some distance between us. I would go to New York. I had some research I planned to do at the Public Library for the Performing Arts, and I would visit my mother. But first I would see my godmother. No matter how far apart my visits to her might be spaced, she never failed to ask me about our theater, what piece we might be working on; what particular themes motivated our explorations. I always assumed her interest to be purely supportive. Too late, at the time of her memorial, I discovered that her first love had been theater, how her family had quashed her desire to become an actress. Among her effects, I discovered a program for a high school play she was directing at the progressive academy where she taught French, a school I had attended in first grade. It was a production of Maurice Maeterlinck's *The Blue Bird*, and I realized how, as a child of six, I had stumbled into the auditorium across the hall from my classroom, and what I had seen in rehearsal there—my first exposure to theater—was the very play, directed by her, whose program I now held in my hands, forty years later.

My mother prepared to receive me every morning with friends of hers in attendance. She held court, tightly corseted, fully armored in bracelets, brooches, earrings, and necklaces. At the time it struck me she wanted them to witness my homage, but looking back, I wonder if somehow she was feeling in need of their protection. I kept my promise to visit her daily during my two-week stay. One day, however, when time ran away from me, I phoned to let her know that I needed to keep to another schedule, promising to pay an extra long visit the following day. But when I phoned ahead, no answer. I waited one day. I phoned again. No answer.

By then she was eighty-four years of age; she lived alone. Her passive-aggressive habits had long been familiar, but it occurred to me I had better pay her a call, appointment or no. I rang her bell. I waited. At last I heard her footsteps approaching along the corridor. The door opened. She was dressed in a wraparound house dress. She wore no corsets, no jewelry. She smiled apologetically. "I thought you were the boy delivering my port." She gazed at me for a moment, felt the need to explain her getup: "I was washing the floor." She pronounced *floor* with that French inflection, *flore*. I knew "washing the floor" was code for "I am so hurt, so angry with you, I could *scream*." I took it all in: this diminutive woman, shrunken with age. Then—quite by impulse—I was wrapping her tiny frame in my arms. Rocking her slightly. "You are something," I whispered, "you are really something." To my astonishment she began making little animal sounds of pure pleasure, little moans of deep and utter satisfaction. I released her.

She removed her rubber gloves. "Come in," she said.

There was never any guarantee that I would ever forgive my mother. There was little chance we would ever reconcile. As a child, subject to constant punishment, I took to warning both my parents that never in my adult life would I ever look after them in their old age. All the more reason to count this as one of the miraculous moments of my life. Perhaps my mother did too. In all probability she had waited for such an event her entire lifetime—and done everything in her power never to enjoy it. Deep down, beneath her armor of corsets and cheap metal ornaments, I recognized how fragile she had become. And how alone. And that I must have cared. Perhaps the lessons of *Eurydice* had moved my heart. Perhaps I was ready to forgive her because I had learned to forgive myself for the many years I held her in contempt. Because deep down love must have spoken louder than history.

It would take me years to examine my bent to favor my father and to despise my mother. Years finally to recognize that, yoked to him, faithful till the end, she had consigned her life to an emotional desert by staying in a marriage that year after year must have withered her heart. In all those years living with an indifferent husband—in complete denial of his sexual preferences—who lavished all his attention on the small girl whose birth she had imagined might become her solace in old age. Yet, despite her cruelty, she had been the one to urge me to "be different." She had been the one to remind me: "You will be a writer!" We never did become "best friends." With her controlling ways, she just wasn't a whole lot of fun to be around, but we both recognized our moment that day when, perhaps for the first time, she must have felt she had a daughter and it felt as though I may have had a mother.

10. Invitation to a Threesomes

With *After Eurydice*, perhaps because of its protracted two-year rehearsal period, something had changed. For one thing, although the piece still bore the signature ritual framework inspired by my work with Paul Rebillot, its originality marked a transition from earlier work. We followed it in 1974 with *Stoneground*, our text inspired by Manuel Mujica Láinez's novel *Bomarzo* (and the subject of a 1962 opera by Alberto Ginastera), whose protagonist Orsini's stronghold borders an Etruscan necropolis. Central to *Stoneground* (staged one year before Vietnam's final debacle) was an interrogation of war-making itself and the readiness of fathers all too willingly to sacrifice their sons. We staged the battle scene with the help of our aikido coach, who trained us in such lightning-swift moves as throws and shoulder rolls. Nude sequences (fig. 10) represented the protagonist's dreams in which the nearby Etruscan necropolis came to life. One of these scenes reached a climax when Orsini's mask was torn off, revealing nothingness. This theme of self-nothingness would reappear later in my fiction.

Stoneground spoke to my own tentative sense of self, and with its reference to the wasteland of war, it reflected a search for a narrative that more closely tapped the zeitgeist. Part of that search would involve considering the work of other theater-makers, and what better place for a representative sampling of avant-garde work than East-

FIG. 10. An ancient Etruscan necropolis comes to life in a dream sequence of *Stoneground*, Theatre of Man's 1974 production. (Courtesy of James Armstrong.)

ern Europe, at that time a place of rich theatrical ferment. I was also keen to see the work of American director Robert Wilson. That year, he had entered *Letter to Queen Victoria*, which ran as part of the Belgrade BITEF Festival.

Through the recommendation of Anne Dennis Yankovic, our theater school's mime instructor, I reached out to her Belgrade contacts. Our theater's portfolio impressed them, but they were utterly dumbfounded when they discovered that Theatre of Man was not government subsidized. "*Privat?!*" they exclaimed, stunned, "*Privat?!?!*" They couldn't get over the shock of it. How could such a thing be? Their theater was fully subsidized, their highly original work was recognized as important, their artists deserving of a living wage. They offered free Thursday afternoon performances for factory-worker audiences who were let off work early to attend. But our work was "*privat?!*" What sort of country did we live in? How could such work survive?

Although Wilson's work was compelling in unexpected ways, ultimately I found it frigid, but I stayed in Belgrade long enough to take in the work of such recognized directors as Andrzej Wajda and to see Branko Pleša's postmodern staging of Aleksandr Sukhovo-Kobylin's grotesquely dystopian *Death of Tarelkin*. I found a gesture of Konrad Swinarski's marking the passage of time to be most memorable. Behind a scrim, in the far up stage, a courting couple slowly passed stage left to right. In act 2 the same couple appeared, still moving stage left to right, the woman visibly pregnant. By the third act, the couple took a last turn stage left to right, wheeling a baby carriage.

My Yugloslav colleagues' question stayed with me. It raised a serious issue. What role should governments play in subsidizing the arts? I was finding that making the kind of theater I had in mind had become increasingly problematic because more favorable conditions seemed to be absent at home. Contemporary American dramatic focus, at least at that time, never seemed to reach much beyond individual lives or dysfunctional families, formulas the American public had come to expect. Observing the theaters of countries whose populations were relatively homogeneous suggested that, for a theater to speak to national aspirations, audiences had to recognize such matters as a shared history, a shared literature and literary tradition, and hold deep cultural and sociopolitical convictions in common.

A few outstanding exceptions come to mind, such as *Mary Dyer Hanged in Boston*, one of Doris Baizley's early plays; *Tom Paine* by Paul Foster; *Angels in America* by Tony Kushner; and of course such classics as *Death of a Salesman* and *The Crucible*, and, more recently adapted for the stage, Sinclair Lewis' tragically prophetic *It Can't Happen Here*. Certainly minority and affinity groups come to mind: the black theater of August Wilson, Langston Hughes, Lorraine Hansberry, and Ntozake Shange among others; the work of El Teatro Campesino; and, still ongoing, the San Francisco Mime Troupe, now in its sixtieth year. But by and large, the public able to support theater with America's high ticket prices could not be described so much an embattled class as a co-opted one.

It may be for that reason theater artists committed to deeply authentic expression, certainly at that particular time, found working in the United States systemically challenging—especially if they intended to survive. Happy exceptions exist to this day: the Bread and Puppet Theater and New York–based Lone Wolf Tribe. And—richly ironic—a 2018 production of Camus' *State of Siege*, staged by Theatre de la Ville, a French company, and reviewed by Charles McNulty of the *Los Angeles Times*, comes closest to exemplifying what an authentic, no-holds-barred native American theater, reflective of our political realities and transcendent of class or race, needs to look like in the present day.

We went into rehearsal for our 1974–1975 season with Kafka's novel *The Trial* as our springboard, not so much to re-create the novel's narrative as to evoke a Kafkaesque world. Contributing to our project's success was a yeasty collaboration that included Bill Young as our composer in residence and Paris-born Michel Indergand, a conceptual artist, as our lighting designer. Initially we started out as a team of four, collaborating with a scenic designer, but he found working with a woman director problematic and resigned. Indergand replaced him.

Our production team discussed what kind of vision might best convey Kafka's world. We saw it as cluttered, rife with uncertainties and the sort of arbitrary incongruities that evoked the matter-of-factness—and anxieties—of dream. Indergand created costuming suggestive of disaster zones: hazard equipment, safety vests, utility gloves, Dietz street warning barricades, rain ponchos, industrial leggings, iron-tipped shoe protectors, aviator's goggles, Plexiglas welder's helmets, rubber waders, and rain jackets. He designed almost all of the lighting to be handheld: cigarette lighters, candles, flashlights (one suitable for flogging), lanterns, and miner's lamps. Improvising with such materials as cargo ropes, butcher paper, corrugated cardboard, strips of burlap, torn sheeting, and a truckload of repurposed fabric rollers, the actors created the automaton world of the office sequences and the labyrinthine spaces of the court. The musical score relied on real-time sounds such as a shot put thundering twenty yards across a suspended wood floor.

We solved the bridging problem between nonverbal and verbal work using some of Kafka's iconic phrases in a simple exercise called *the phrase*. It was an approach that served me well when later I turned to fiction. Most of the sections of *Face*, my debut novel, could be said to be driven by the motor of an opening phrase. Some examples from *The Trial* might include:

> This way...
> Keep to the wall...
> It won't be long...
> The bell hasn't even rung!!!!
> You must have made a mistake...
> Feel your way...
> It's dark in here...

But the process of putting the various elements together to create a performance work such as Theatre of Man's *Trial*, combining text, choreographic elements, costumes, lighting, sound, and a musical component, is not what an audience sees. What rivets them to their seats is the image of suppliants massed in the subterranean recesses of the court of law, dragging dilapidated folding chairs across the space, lashed together by cargo ropes. Some, barely able to walk, propping themselves on canes (those repurposed fabric rollers), leaning on one another, exhausted by years of defeat at the hands of a system of justice designed to confuse and confound all those whose lifelong search is to seek remedy.

Our actual performance venue came equipped with two-by-four framing, staircases, and platforms, allowing us to create a nest of stages with connecting staircases able to accommodate simultaneous scenes on three different levels. All the while intercutting lines of text, the nurse, Leni, could feed Block dinner; K's uncle Max could intercede with the lawyer in his sickbed (fig. 11); the clerk of the court, dressed in a nightshirt, could quite casually sit up in the bed beside him; and across the way, artists' models lit by handheld candelabra could appear in ceremonial drag as stand-ins for the judges.

Reflecting a world turned upside-down, a reconfigured staging arrangement reversed the space, with the audience seated on risers

FIG. 11. Tom Macaulay as Uncle Max visits Huld, the lawyer (Mark Carmichael), as Leni (Laurie Hoffman) looks on in Theatre of Man's 1975 production of *The Trial*. (Courtesy of Michael Bry.)

within the theater's proscenium and the action unfolding deep into the actual auditorium, with K's final exit through the doors actually marked EXIT into the corridor ninety feet beyond.

One reviewer wrote, "By showing us our world in surreal form, Theatre of Man presents a reflection of our real world. The doubt, alienation, absurdity, paranoia, bureaucratic insanity, anxiety, and helplessness are all there ... making our nightmare realities visible." Our season saw a box office success rivaling that of *Murder in the Cathedral*, but federal support still eluded us. To obtain it we would have had to offer a minimum number of performances, but to offer that many required a federal grant.

Among its other distinctions, that season was the closest our company ever came to obtaining National Endowment support. Scout recommenders from the NEA (who are supposed to remain anonymous) attended one of *Trial*'s performances. In keeping with protocol, they avoided introducing themselves to me. I watched passively as they left, their hands tucked amicably in each other's back pockets. Throughout our twelve-year history, we remained *privat*.

In May we took *The Trial* down and stored the lights and props in the basement of our newly acquired performance space, a little-used parish hall located in Haight-Ashbury, one block down from my family's original San Francisco flat. It was unimproved in every way. The foyer, separated by a pair of French doors, was perfectly suited for use as a green room, a space where actors could temporarily leave the rehearsal floor and where ordinary everyday social interaction could take place. It would come to serve handily as the entrance foyer on performance nights. The suspended wood floor made it suitable as a rehearsal and performance venue, and compared to our concrete slab rehearsal loft, it was certainly more friendly to bare feet. But it was a floor in need of a good sanding and refinishing.

At this point, one of our actors who had worked with our company three seasons in a row, paid me a visit. Hardscrabble, intermittently incarcerated since the age of twelve, he looked to me as something of a mother figure. "Now you have a space," he warned me, "all your energies will go toward maintaining it. Your artistic work will pay the price." That visit would be the last I would ever see of him.

Day Seven

U.S. immigration policy reflects the xenophobia that still characterizes a country whose policies originate in the desire to keep its population homogeneous, white, and Protestant. Quotas established in 1921 and 1924 made it evident that immigrants from Northern and Western Europe (white and for the most part Protestant) were favored over those from the south and east (darker, Catholic and Jewish) whose entry was seen as "illegal," setting a dangerous precedent and facilitating the rise of the infrastructure that continues today to identify, apprehend, and deport so-called illegal aliens.

From its inception, the culture of institutions charged with enforcing deportation is a brutal one. From the first state laws targeting the poor and the "dangerous" in 1794 to the Indian Removal Act that expelled

First Nations people from their own lands as if they were foreign nationals, it is a policy that has been characterized by the racism that selects for white and discriminates against persons of color, be they Chinese, barred from the United States under the Chinese Exclusion Act of 1882, which stayed in effect till its repeal in 1943, or the Mexican and southern European Bisbee strikers expelled in 1917 (the first time American citizens were expelled). It set another dangerous precedent, preparing the stage for the imprisonment of Japanese Americans, approximately 110,000 of whom were incarcerated during World War II.

But the history of Mexican deportation, beginning in 1924, became a wave in 1931 through 1938, when 1.8 million people, many of them American citizens, were deported under the euphemism of "repatriation" in an operation that today could only be described as "racial cleansing." Subsequently the United States deported another three hundred thousand Mexicans in 1958 when "Operation Wetback" colluded with farm employers to exploit migrant workers by creating versions of the Bracero Program that scaled back benefits for those Mexican workers who participated.*

After 9/11, the targeting of Muslims became the new national pastime. In his affidavit of December 12, 2005, Shayana Kadidal of the Center for Constitutional Rights even states: "Muslim male immigration detainees of South Asian or Arab descent were . . . all denied access to attorneys, phone calls, and bond. They were frequently detained for months after their final deportation orders for the purposes of criminal investigation and were repeatedly and unnecessarily strip-searched; one of our clients . . . despite being held in solitary confinement, was strip- and cavity-searched before entering an immigration judge's courtroom, and, absurdly, strip- and cavity-searched upon leaving that same courtroom. Dogs were systematically used to intimidate Muslim detainees, especially at the Passaic . . . facility where many were held." Both the use of dogs and the systematic use of nudity as a form of humiliation mirrored tactics used at Auschwitz during the Third Reich

---

* See Francisco E. Balderrama and Raymond Rodriguez, *Decade of Betrayal: Mexican Repatriation in the 1930s*.

and later copied by the United States not only domestically but at Abu Ghraib and Guantanamo.

Before its formalization, deportation in the United States, particularly targeting Mexicans, displayed the same xenophobic mentality as ICE's chilling final orders of removal. According to Senator Frank L. Dunn's 2004 investigation, the so-called repatriations of 1931–1938, which resulted in the deportation of 1.8 million Mexicans from areas as far apart as Michigan, New York, Texas, and California, picked up people indiscriminately, undocumented and citizens alike, and harassed them out of the country. Mass raids and arrests were conducted without warrants. Deportees were held incommunicado, forbidden to see anyone or to post bail, and jailed until the next deportation train could be scheduled. C. P. Visel, spokesperson for the Los Angeles Citizens Committee for Coordination of Unemployment Relief, telegraphed: "Four thousand deportable alien [Mexicans] U.S. Estimate 5% [here alone.] We can pick them all up through police and sheriff channels.... Advise please as to method of getting rid. We need their jobs for needy citizens." Many organizations, including the American Federation of Labor, Veterans of Foreign Wars, the American Legion, the National Club of America for Americans, and media outlets, including the Hearst newspapers and the *Saturday Evening Post*, supported their deportation en masse. A House bill called for establishing concentration camps for any alien subject to deportation, another called for deportation of any and all aliens who, in those Depression years, had become public charges. A third called for deportation of all aliens convicted of crimes involving "moral turpitude." Racial profiling ran rampant; acting first, questioning later became policy. City police, county sheriffs, all cooperated with federal agents to stage full-scale military operations. Arrests were made without warrant or cause other than the excuse that "people looked Mexican."

The likelihood of being swept up kept people, especially those concentrated in the barrios, in terror, particularly in Los Angeles, where scare tactics encouraged both legal and illegal residents to leave. Children were kept out of school, shopping was conducted at night, and in general people avoided going out unless absolutely necessary. In high-profile raids, people were lined up and asked to show their papers. Those unable to produce them were detained. Despite their objections, any bystanders who moved to interfere had their own documents seized and withheld. Children were left behind to fend for themselves.

In the present day, deportees are expelled with little more than the shirts on their backs. In a letter from Kingston Jamaica dated August 2, 2005, detainee Barry Walker writes: "When they gave me the flight paper[s] on Friday July 29, they took me straight to the airport with no notice [even] to get any clothes or money together."

Unlike Walker, who was repatriated to Jamaica, many deportees are sent back to a region or a country that is altogether unknown to them. They arrive in an unfamiliar airport with no money and no resources that might allow them to make contact with their distant families.

I joined an organized theater trip to Poland. Late in Prime Minister Wojciech Jaruzelski's protracted term of office, the political atmosphere in Poland had relaxed sufficiently for the once-banned work of Bruno Schulz to come to popular notice; a theater in Wrocław actually produced a work loosely based on *The Street of Crocodiles*, Schulz's dystopian work of magic realism, and at the time of my visit, a five-thousand-copy print run of a first edition of *Księga Listów*, a compendium of his correspondence and rather louche drawings sold out in less than a week.

In Poland I was exposed to the work of such auteurs as Tadeusz Kantor, Jerzy Grotowski, and Józef Szajna. After seeing Szajna's work, I proposed a cultural exchange with him that would allow American audiences to see one of his epic projects such as *Don Quixote* while bringing *Trial* to Europe. Sznajna met my proposal with "You beautiful voman. You bed me?" There were to be no cultural exchanges that year.

A trial of a more personal sort awaited me at home. I had begun to recognize that our marriage was coming to an end. My sense that my work had become highly skilled better prepared me to meet it, but I still failed to see how my five-year state of denial amounted to an abdication. Felix pleaded unmet needs. By way of explanation he offered examples of housewives in our circle faithfully serving their doctor husbands, comfortable in their subsidiary roles, cooking, cleaning, and making appointments. I could only point out that in all the years of rehearsal and performance, I still attended to our family's well-being; that having my own work was my way to growth, and growth was what life must be about; that it was necessary to struggle every year to destroy what came before in order to create anew. I felt I was pleading for my life.

Perhaps the late-found recognition of our needs for autonomy might have allowed us a true marriage, but time was not kind: just as we had begun to negotiate, our time came to an end. A journal excerpt a week before our separation seems telling:

> At the end, my feelings have become more stabilized. I see that I face the classic conflict of sending away the person I love most dearly. But when all is said, it's good for me to be on my own.... There's a book here somewhere, or a theater piece. A work that would have to do with disenfranchisement and the *myth of being nobody*.

There was little hope of reconciliation. I filed for divorce. Within six months, I had an interlocutory decree; within a year, when the divorce was final, my lawyer treated me to a celebratory breakfast of eggs Florentine at the San Francisco Palace Hotel. She was a good lawyer, one of three I'd interviewed. The first, a man, was quick to point out that with my earnings history, I could hardly expect any alimony to speak of. I picked a woman because her first question to me was "Tell me about your aspirations for yourself and your children." Once I'd finished, she remarked, "I can understand why you care for him so much, and why you feel bereft." The other reason was that occupying her desk in a place of prominence was a Kleenex box.

Although the formalities ended within months, it would take me years fully to come to terms with this, one of my life's major watersheds. But through it all, we mostly managed to conduct ourselves with relative decency. I must have spent most of that first year in a bathrobe, an indication that on certain days, although I managed to get up, I hardly remember doing much else, but for the first time in my life I had more than allowance money at my disposal: alimony, child support, and a San Francisco house, now in my name. The child support would end as our sons reached eighteen years of age, but alimony—well-meaning people assured me—would run forever or end with demise, mine or his, or remarriage, mine—whichever came first. Friends helped me live through a year of what felt like devastating grief. Rage and anger too. But what exactly was that grief? Had my marriage been a placeholder after all, a safe territory where, protected by its mask, I could take the risks I felt my work required?

How would my sons feel if I were to take back my given name? They gave the question some thought. Their verdict came back. No, they would like to feel they had two parents, not just one. They were young, too young to see their father leave. I honored their request, and once again, I deferred the opportunity to reconnect my true name to my origins.

I took a roommate. Rose had worked for the theater as our stage manager. She knew the house, having housesat for us. My sons helped in the sense that I felt obliged to be of some comfort to them and to provide them with a sense of continuity, for I imagined their loss to be even greater than my own. The reason Rose was there, more than anything, was to spare them from having to listen to my resentments. It was a fair exchange: Rose had abundant resentments of her own.

Before it could become a performance venue, our rehearsal hall would need equipment: risers, blacks, a grid and light board, and a sound system. Funds were needed, volunteer labor needed to be lined up and scheduled from among the students attending our theater school. And there was that hardwood floor that could use a sanding. I ran to it like a lover. I could still raise funds, organize volunteer work crews, and refinish a floor, but I was not prepared to direct ever again. I believed I had lost the edge, the fool's courage I imagined my marriage had provided me—as if somehow I had borrowed my father's circumventions only to see them cruelly explode.

John Parkinson, one of our acting school instructors, proposed I write a Medea, which he volunteered to direct the following season. Medea, a theme appropriate to an abandoned wife. But wait! What version of Medea?

From the beginning, his-story's project seems to have been to rewrite history. Was there another story—before the patriarchy took root? According to Robert Graves, the pre-Euripidean version had it that, far from sacrificing her two sons out of vengeance, the Corinthians stoned Medea's twenty-three children to death. The Corinthian city fathers actually bribed Euripides to come up with the patriarchal version that's come down to us. According to Graves, the pre-classic Medea was actually forced to flee, finding refuge in the cities of Asia Minor, then forced to flee again, a legend that suggests patriarchy was vying for dominance, destroying the shrines of the earth goddess one by one throughout the Middle East.

Happily, the *Medea* I delivered has never seen publication. Like much early work, it falls short, a clumsy attempt to tell a complicated story. An awkward text and stiff direction would ensure it arrived DOA, but to this day, the story of suppressed histories is one I find compelling. I would discover how much it happens to be my own.

A year had elapsed, a year of prowling the night streets of San Francisco, scanning third-story windows, in the warmth of their inviting glow grieving the loss of my own hearth. Once I even caught sight of an Indian hanging nearly identical to my own, but it showed a full moon, while mine depicted the darkness of a new moon night.

A wild impulse propelled me. Before our divorce, my mother-in-law had hoped she might retire in San Francisco close to us, "in a little house, with no hills, close to a supermarket," but when the time came, she greeted the announcement of our dissolution with an "I told you so." Although I barely had five thousand dollars to my name, my sons had each saved up equal amounts. I would borrow from them and another five thousand from her for three years at no interest. I picked a realtor from the yellow pages. The next afternoon he showed me three properties. I bought the third, a pair of flats with a south garden—a small one not requiring much maintenance, two or three level blocks from a supermarket. Twenty thousand down secured the loan. The deal closed, although in the absence of any credit history of my own, a friend had to cosign for me, but when I handed my ex-mother-in-law the keys, she stayed unimpressed. My feelings of triumph fell flat. I rented the flats. Within six months, I had repaid my sons; I sent my mother-in-law the final payment three years later to the day.

At first, alimony payments made carrying two mortgages possible, but three years later, they came to a sudden halt. My lawyer agreed to see us both. I waited for Felix in a small anteroom next to her office. When I saw him arrive, even in profile, I could see things had not gone well with him. I thought it over. There was only one solution. I had no sense of how I might manage alone, but when we sat down to lunch, I released him from any obligation to support me. In retrospect it was the best thing I'd ever done. I'd be on my own. I'd carry my two mortgages working two jobs back to back—a one-year stint that had me falling asleep at the dinner table. It had to end. I sold the property, in four years quadrupling my initial investment—our investment. My sons had helped to make our gains possible. I parlayed our gains by taking back a note.

Using property as collateral to secure loans to buy more property used to be called pyramiding. Over the next fifteen years, at a time when the dollar still had purchasing power, I returned to pyramiding. During the remainder of my productive life, my irrational impulse, undertaken in the mistaken assumption that by benefiting an ex-mother-in-law I might somehow restore a broken family, would become an unexpected source of freedom. I would no longer need to rent out my time or energy to someone other than myself or depend on someone to support me. It would afford me the time I needed—once I understood how much I needed it—to do the work I do. And best of all, my words would always be my own, impervious to commercial or ideological constraints. But this latter perception would dawn on me only much later.

For the time being, I was still a theater-maker. Thessalonians came calling in the person of three frustrated actors, Tom Macaulay, a comic actor, and star of *Trial*; Mary Tepper, a dramatic actress, who had starred in *Stoneground*; and Greg Wagers, also from *Trial*, a metaphysical actor. All three urged me to give them something into which to sink their teeth. I would be working with two men and one woman, not the usual fifteen to nineteen actors as had been my wont, but each inhabited a very separate sensibility. The problem was how best to make a piece to contain them.

We began improvising with all kinds of objects: clothing, hats, basketballs, butcher paper, rope, a red plastic bat, an army-surplus parachute, and pots and pans, the more dented, the better. As our rehearsals progressed, one might relate to a certain improvisation, the other two not so much. In the process, each began shaping a defined persona. As they declared themselves, I sensed the comedic potential in each. We had a clown show on our hands: Greg as Whiteface, the passive-aggressive clown whose machinations foment nothing but trouble; Mary as Auguste, awkward and oversized, battling the towering burdens stacked against her; and Tom as the Tramp, the eternal innocent, not quite committed to reality.

I commissioned sculptor Nancy Worthington to create three nests: for Mary, a kind of elaborate jungle gym from which she could hold forth or hang upside down as she battled the elements; for Greg, suspended from the rafters by a cargo net a rebar cage in which he could brood; and for Tom, a kind of aardvark nest whose runway consisted of a long and blistered tongue. Alternating with sadistic little games (fig. 12), each clown took separate turns. We called it *Threesomes*, and at last we had a theater of our own, a fully equipped black box in which to stage it.

One critic wrote: "The actors refer to each other by their given names; there are no 'roles' in *Threesomes*, nor is there a plot. There is structure, however, but it's ... in the nature of a phrase-pattern, more like a symphony than a drama.... It's a rare experience to leave the theater harboring the impulse to think." Audiences came. Some left baffled; others laughed themselves silly; still others lingered, wanting to delay their departure by talking with the company. I never met them. When the lights came up, I hid. *Threesomes* was unlike anything I had ever made before. Its essentially modernist approach where the performer was placed directly before the audience in all his personal authenticity replaced my previous ritual style, but the piece left me feeling as though I'd widely missed the mark. Like the aftermath of some catastrophe, the space looked like it could use a power wash. It

FIG. 12. "Alternating with sadistic little games." Tom Macaulay as "Tom" and Greg Wagers as "Greg" in Theatre of Man's 1977 production of *Threesomes*. (Courtesy of John Parkinson.)

would take us nearly an hour to stow all the props for the following night's performance. Why would anyone want to stay and talk? There was nothing left to say. And yet...

And yet. In the final scene of *Threesomes*, Mary's temporary absence from her nest prompted Tom to help himself to her hoard of stash, while in Tom's absence, Greg stripped him bare, while Mary ripped off everything of Greg's she could possibly carry, and unable to carry any more, grabbed his red plastic bat in her teeth. The piece ended with a pensive Greg, perched in his cage, musing: "You hang by a thread... [pause]... You know where you are."

Fast forward to our kleptomaniac age: bankers ripping off marginalized home owners with subprime mortgages, Enron ripping off its stakeholders and the California Independent System Operator for billions of dollars, corporations ripping off taxpayers for toxic site cleanup, vulture capitalists feeding on a postdisaster world, and Florida's hanging chad debacle, with planeloads of mobsters flying in at Halliburton's expense to paralyze the 2000 vote recount, which gave the world George Bush and the invasion of Afghanistan and Iraq under false flag pretenses—a threesome of corporations, government, and financial institutions operating a daisy chain of rip-offs.

It has taken me years to recognize that the production my disappearance tried so utterly to disown may have been our most original work to date, the one that came closest to tapping the zeitgeist. Although I had no way of knowing it at the time, this strange little hybrid was to be the last performance piece I would ever put before a public.

11. Zigzagging with Goya

A month after the *Threesomes* run ended in May 1977, the *San Francisco Chronicle* ran a fill piece on the last page of Section A: "Man Reconstructs Own Face." Refused surgical help after a catastrophic facial accident, Walter Alves Pereira managed to rebuild his own face, with one of Brazil's foremost plastic surgeons volunteering to intervene at last at his own personal expense. The story hammered at me, exactly why I had no time to fathom, but in it I recognized the makings of a powerful work of fiction—for someone who had time. I made sure I was too busy, but I tacked the clip to my bulletin board to ensure it wouldn't run away.

That fall I went into rehearsal with the *Threesomes* company, improvising around the theme of time passing. We called our work-in-progress *Time/Piece*. Although we made some headway developing a performance score, possibly because the theme we hoped to address, family dysfunction, still lacked my own necessary clarity, the project failed to coalesce. Undeterred, I went into rehearsal the following season with a project titled *Goya*. I had been pondering the images of *Los Caprichos* and *The Horrors of War*, reading Francisco de Goya biographies to connect them somehow with the fugue episode in Goya's forty-third year (I was the same age at the time), when, as the royal tapestry designer, he was encouraged to turn out designs of rosy-cheeked maidens reading love letters or receiving the attentions of their swains—the pinups of his day—but gradually, overcome with self-disgust, he must have cried *Basta!* and fled Madrid for Malaga—as far away from the court as it was possible to get.

As he traveled the rutted roads by stagecoach, he succumbed to a paralyzing illness. I imagined him falling out of that stage into the receiving arms of his friend, Dr. Martinez, numb and unable to speak, and at year's end, relearning how to walk, climb stairs, and speak once more, but with the faculty of hearing lost to him forever—his way perhaps of turning a deaf ear to the continued blandishments of his king. It was a leave-taking that struck me as a watershed.

I felt prompted to explore my own leave-takings: from my father, and later from my theater mentor—the necessary step any artist needs to take before declaring herself, and maybe something else too, something not yet obvious to me. I began rehearsals in collaboration with Roger Berry, a solar sculptor. One of our first exercises was to supply ear plugs to the company—to all of us—and to visit Lands End, to experience the power of the tide, wave after wave, as it rolled in without a sound.

Berry supplied an array of objects and materials, some of them taken directly from the images of the *Los Caprichos*: mops and broomsticks, bloodied baby dolls in wicker baskets, buckets, and a two-man saw, which he suspended from the rafters. Two especially gifted actresses, Yaffa Corteen and Linda Grznar, became part of the company, totaling three men and three women, who came to represent actual people in Goya's waking life, and they reappeared in the dream sequences in a kind of *bardo* in which they became transformed into the shadows of his tortured psyche.

As we worked, images began to form. Flour sacks stuffed with goose down became Goya's sick bed, his huge frame composed of the actors themselves: head, torso, and four extremities, coming gradually to life. One of the most startling gestures ever invented by an actress—at least in my experience—came from Linda Grznar: suspended upside down from the rafters, she slid her tongue along the naked blade of Berry's two-man saw.

Collective creation such as was our practice may very well be the most volatile approach to making theater, and for this reason, most of our rehearsals were closed. But *Goya*'s fate may already have been compromised, when in the midst of rehearsals, I remembered my bulletin board. It was certainly large and material enough not to have evaporated, and not surprisingly, still pinned to it was the clip from the May 1977 *San Francisco Chronicle*.

As we continued exploring the theme of leave-taking, our exercises drew on the actors' personal lives; one actor excused his absence with a dental visit, followed by yet another dental visit, because finally, the work evoked such disturbing life associations, he needed to substitute the denial of toothache for honest paralysis. And that is what happened to Goya: one of his limbs went numb. We had come to a place where, because the actors were only six in number, the piece was no longer viable. I saw no other way. I closed the project, much to everyone's regret. It was my way of saying, *Basta!* a decision that cost the company dear. But there was a reason I felt I had somewhat less at stake. Sparked by that clip from the *San Francisco Chronicle*, I had begun writing something. I had no idea where it might take me. And still unaware, I was in the midst of yet another leave-taking, this one from the theater. It felt like a devastating loss, the collapse of something on which I'd wagered my identity.

Once Reagan came to power, however meager to begin with, funding for the arts, and in particular my company, began drying up. Two theater projects in a row had failed to coalesce; my twenty-year marriage had collapsed. With no pressing obligations left, neither to a marriage nor to my work, I began to feel my life was showing some reluctance to turn out well. Nights of sleeplessness stretched into weeks. It must have been around that time that lying suspended in the dark, lost in some hypnogogic state, something unusual happened to me. In my mind's eye, a woman appeared, bending over me with all the tenderness and grace of a mother, a woman whose features were blank, but whose dark hair framed her face. Who? Who might she have been?

It occurred to me I must be warding off a dream wanting to surface. The night was chill. I threw on an extra sweater, made my way down two flights of stairs. At that hour there was something raw about my study's naked light. It searched out too much of my disorder, but I resisted the temptation to put everything to rights. I sat at my typewriter instead, pondering the keys. Slowly a story ("End of the Road") took shape, the first of a number of Bruno stories, none of them published, that inhabit some grim Eastern European city where the sun never shines. An evacuation order is posted. Crowds of refugees braving the icy winds line up at the street car lines. Baffled children huddle in doorways, their scarves wrapped high about their eyes.

With just time to slip his pen and notebook in his pocket, Bruno takes to the stairs leading to the street. He races toward the depot, but just past the Place of the Theater, a fall leaves him stunned, sprawled out in the gutter, unable to move until long after the last transport has left. Slowly he begins making his way through the eerie, deserted streets, heading for the bridge leading to the wooded countryside beyond. At dawn the following morning, from across the river, he catches sight in the distance of his city burning, clouds of smoke dissipating ashes into the wintry air.

Aimlessly he wanders the forest, churning up the fallen leaves. A wolf trap springs. He's caught at last, unable to move. He spends his days, notebook in hand, recording temperatures and wind velocity. At last a stage crew finds his body. With a kick the foreman turns it over to make sure he's dead. "Get working," he shouts. One by one, the crew hook the trees to the guy ropes. "Take 'er up!" shouts the foreman. As the trees disappear into the flies, his laughter is lost in the grating of the stage machinery.

III

Making Words

12. Consultation with a Sibyl

My life in the theater had come to an end, but I didn't go without a fight. Not a psychic, not a palmist certainly, Jean Palmer must have been a sibyl, an oracle perhaps, her name given me by my colleague Norah Holmgren of the Firehouse Theater, the only other woman stage director working in San Francisco at that time. I brought her my questions: Would I find some way to reconnect with my work? Would I ever remarry? At the time I hadn't quite realized how linked both questions were in my mind. I sat quietly waiting for her response. She positioned herself at right angles to me. Eyes closed, tapping her right foot rhythmically on the floor, panting through one open nostril while blocking the other, she seemed to go into something of a trance. At last she spoke.

"Before you can come to any answers, you need to look at your relationship with your father," she told me. "He plays a significant role in your story. He wanted somehow to keep you in a place where you wouldn't be able to leave. He was afraid that, like a moth, you might be drawn to the light. He put you somewhere where there were windows, but where the screens made escape impossible."

I was more than curious to know how and where she might have acquired a skill so remarkable that, without having any previous knowledge of me or my life, she was able to put her finger on such a pressure point. She let me know she'd worked with Peter Schumann for a number of years, but regardless, her words left me with more questions than before.

I recalled that, five years prior, a newly divorced friend had returned from Paris with her children—four of them—in tow. Panicked that within six months she would have to become their sole support, she consulted a psychiatrist, who guided her through a quick-fix process called "divorcing mom and dad." Hilda Burton was her name.

I had been warned Burton was tough, so tough I was once moved to tell her she reminded me of a Sherman tank. She once asked me if I didn't feel like a fraud. At the time, I had no idea how a fraud might feel, but she saw through my self-deceptions, and one by one, she leveled her guns to take them down. Maybe Felix had exploited me, but our relationship had been reciprocally exploitative. Self-awakening came as a shock.

We might have gotten around to having a look at my childhood, except that I had been able to afford her fee only because I was drawing alimony, and now suddenly it had dried up, and without that financial support I would have to find work and find it at once. I needed to bring our visits to a close. She insisted I wasn't ready to discharge myself, not by a long shot. She suggested I would have to take a serious look at myself first. I felt I understood what needed to be done. What I heard her say was that if I were to make any headway, a radical personality restructuring was in order, but I hadn't the least notion how to go about it.

Four years later, when I had published my debut novel, *Face* (Viking-Penguin, 1985), I would convey some of that dawning awareness.

> Carefully he props the piece of mirror against the wall. In it he studies what he sees there. Calmly, for the first time, he forces his eyes to take the measure of his mangled face. Have the traces of his mother's dying come back to shape his dreams: the dusty bottles, the matches? the syringe?
>
> Where has it come from, this idea? has it hovered for some time, like the dust particles suspended in the sickroom air?

He would make himself a face. He did not have to wait. He would make it here, where he knew no one, where no one could tell him how he had to look, what he had to be—now that he had fallen—now he no longer belonged, even to himself.

Now I had the time to write, and, mapped on a story of a man reconstructing his own face, I had every hope the novel would make enough to guarantee my godmother, who was aging, would never die in penury. I had no way yet of imagining how it might change my life.

Throughout my postgraduate years, my reading had continued to gravitate to international fiction, which led me eventually to discover Kobo Abe, an experimental theater-maker and novelist working in Tokyo. His novel *Woman in the Dunes* dispensed with the predictability of plot by throwing away the climax, forcing him to invent alternative ways for readers to keep the pages turning. I was particularly drawn to his indeterminate ending. In composing *Face* I hoped to put both devices to use. Minimally, I set myself some kind of schedule. I would attempt one small section per day, usually writing before first light, when the day's distractions began to intervene. I faced a blank wall. When time allowed, I drove to Lands End, perching on the rocks above the surf, watching—*becoming*—the play of light as wave upon wave broke on the shore—the place I first found freedom as a child.

My alimony had suddenly dried up, I needed to look for work, and having done the apparently useless business of art, finding paying work would not be easy. Nonprofit sector jobs were scarce and, compared to the corporate world, the pay scale far reduced. But, given my résumé, it was to the nonprofit sector I would turn. There was also a fully equipped theater space now that could be rented to dance and theater companies as a performance venue, but to support my family and carry two mortgages I would have to work two jobs back to back.

To make the employment rounds, I acquired a "dress-for-success" outfit, the first—and last—of a lifetime. After six months of making the rounds, peddling a souped-up résumé, Larry Campbell of Performing Arts Services hired me. Although I suspect he was undeceived by what it contained, the suit may have cinched the deal. He came with the strength to tolerate difference—and the office possessed state-of-the-art technology: a memory typewriter! If I arrived by 8:00 a.m., I could put in one hour of committing my handwritten words to type. I began:

> In the sky a cloud is forming. The head, the shoulders appear. It is May. There is a leaden gray outline lifting the white of the clouds in relief. The blue of the sky is cold, wintry. There is a greenish cast to the light. The sun is absent.
>
> A wind forms across the bay. The expanse of water marks its restlessness in the apparently static crests and troughs. From this distance, the waves appear not to move—curls arrested on a tightly coiffed head. They do not move at all. Looking, then looking away, then rapidly looking again, one can only seem to catch a movement, more imperceptible than breath itself. Or perhaps the waves are the same, the same crests as before. Or perhaps they have only moved one trough closer to the shore, like stop frames shifting slightly in a view finder.
>
> In the sky, the cloud has changed now. The head is lowered, or perhaps it has turned around, or the shoulders have risen to ward off a blow. No more. The giant is gone. Other shapes are forming.

Although the words are never explicit, that colossal cloud and the giant reference might equally be to Goya's painting *The Colossus* or to a mushroom cloud. But those first words provided the energy I came to think of as an opening salvo, an overture packed with enough staying power to hold my hand and see me through. But through what? Three years of composition? There were no assurances.

By then my sons (fig. 13) were striking out, heading to rock concerts, baking Alice B. Toklas cakes to heighten the experience. From where that evening's cake lay on the cooling rack I snatched a bite. My sweet tooth craved another. I took two. And for the devilry of it, I scrounged a third piece from its navel.

"Holy cow!" as my son took the stairs, he sounded the alarm: "That stuff's gonna hit when you're home alone!" He understated his case

FIG. 13. "By then my sons were striking out." David (*left*) and Michael (*right*).

because when the munchies hit, it was not so much a trip as it was like a rocket shot to Saturn—which as it happened, took place that very weekend. Ten days of it, taking leave of my senses, in disheartening mimicry of my breakdown twelve years before.

I showed up at work pie-eyed. "Oh my," my new boss, Larry Campbell, exclaimed half in disbelief. Evidently it was dawning on him he'd hired a flake. "Oh my!" That morning he needed to go to the bank. Given my sorry state, he suggested I might as well tag along.

The bank walls served as a kind of art gallery. I found one of the images riveting—an overhead perspective of a cupola, and peering through its opening gazed a gigantic colorless eye.

> The dome high above him is lurching. He watches it turn slowly, gathering speed, a huge wheel of a hundred spokes, spinning. Through the opening at the apex of the dome, an eye, vast, pale, empty of color is peering down at him. He tries to still the roaring in his ears. It seems to him as though people are lifting him, raising him up. He is passing over them, above their upraised hands. Swaying with them as they rock to the chant.

Although not stated explicitly, these lines from *Face* signal the transformative moment when, still unaware, the protagonist's path turns toward self-liberation.

I worried that my sons had to stand by as they had twelve years before, watching me dissolve. When I showed no sign of coming down, I decided to fly to Los Angeles to stay with friends, some of the time in the company of photographer Lou Stoumen, a companion at the time. By then I had come back down to earth. I read to him from the manuscript in its early stages. "Major," he liked to say "Major!" His Hollywoodese couldn't quite convince me, but eventually, in a bow to his encouragement, three of his photographic images (a barber chasing a cat, two men loading a pig onto truck, an infant lying naked in a crib) found their way into the novel's setting.

Some time later when I accompanied him on a trip to New York, he shot portraits of my godmother, now a shut-in at eighty-nine, no longer able to climb the subway stairs, too panicked by money worries to call the New York cab that might have taken her to The New School, where she could have continued teaching the French theater she so loved, concentrating on the works of Genet, Ionesco, and Beckett. Instead, she kept to her comfortable chair for hours on end, unable to read for failing sight. "But oh, Cecile, now I know why they made us memorize so much in school. I can recite whole poems by heart." And she launched into what must surely be the most poignant poem of exile ever, Charles d'Orléans' "Le Temps a Laissé Son Manteau" (the wind spread his winter coat/of sleet, of rain and snow), marking his long years of captivity during the Hundred Years' War.

We visited my mother. Having withstood a mugging on a noontime New York street, she'd decided to retreat to a retirement community some distance from New York City. I brought her flowers. She had become very frail; her eyes were failing. While I sewed buttons on some of her clothing, she sat appraising me through the owlish glasses that magnified her eyes.

"Are you rich?" she wanted to know. "Do you think you'll ever remarry?" I was not rich. But for the time being I was comfortable. I had sold my San Francisco flats. I was buying second mortgages, lending money at a usurious 22 percent interest—the going rate at the time. And no, the chances were I would never remarry. Perhaps the disguise of yet another assumed name was a need that seemed finally to have deserted me. She showed no sign either of approval or disapproval, but I knew: that move long ago to remove the birthmark that would have marred a décolletage, her repeated admonishments to me when I turned thirteen: "You don't have to show every boy how smart you are." Her expectation must have been I'd marry well and redeem her genteel poverty.

There was never a more authentic time between us than on one of our last visits when I took her out of doors and wheeled her through the grounds. We circled the spreading copper beech that occupied a central spot on the lawn of the residence roundabout. I paused the wheelchair, reached up into the lowest branch, and picked one leaf. It was color of oxblood, its veins thinned to disappearance at leaf's edge. I placed it in her hand. For a long time she examined it. I imagined her old eyes tracing every vein, absorbed in a world that still held meaning for her. Did she see in them a reminder of the leaves and flowers she painted in her botany notebook (fig. 14) long ago, the carefully wrought work of a young girl describing the life of plants? Perhaps she rediscovered in their tracing her mother's orchard, and the mountain meadows where she ran free, reminders of a time when childhood offered its promises to her. More than any words we spoke, more than the small gestures of mending her clothes or replacing her buttons, this one exchange is what I remember best, a moment of agreement, stronger for its wordlessness but charged with a feeling so deep it didn't need a name.

I had never really understood who my mother was. Her shadow passes through these pages no more solid than a wraith's. But all bear through life one central, great, and bottomless grief—the lifepain at the heart of things. Now, when I ponder what burden she must have carried, I am taken back to her own childhood in Switzerland, where she was born, to her earliest memory, a fleeting instance in her baby carriage with her mother wheeling her. As they pass a wayside shrine of the crucified Christ, she tells her mother, "Poor Jesus. Let's put him in the baby carriage."

My mother must have been the oldest because her sister, Blanche, has not yet arrived on the scene. Blanche with her raven black hair and her astonishingly periwinkle eyes must have been younger,

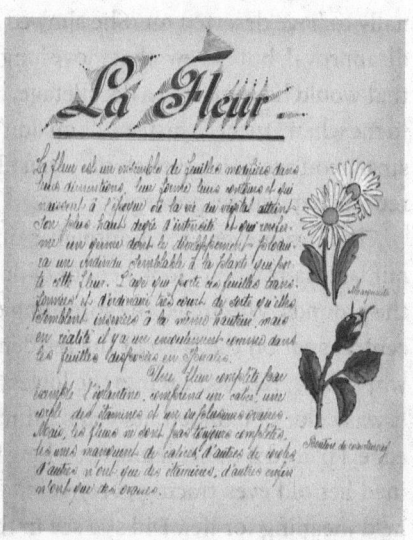

FIG. 14. "Did she see in them a reminder of the leaves and flowers she painted?" My mother's 1901 Botanique.

my mother's little sister, her own little "baby." And when Blanche died at the age of twelve, it must have left my mother with an emptiness that lasted all her life; to add to that loss, not many years later another sister, that one still in infancy, Babette, also died, as had Blanche, of diphtheria. Loss must have left her inconsolable at heart, unable to love a substitute for fear that if she were to love it, it might die, yet in her early days, she had worked as a governess, a very high-end au pair charged with mentoring children—the children of the rich. I remember in early childhood that time when she took me visiting, and when Giffy opened her front door how she called my mother "Maddy!" as she wrapped her in her arms. Perhaps my mother had known the grace of loving someone else's children even if she couldn't love her own.

Sometimes—though rarely—when she forgot herself, she would call me Babette. She had to be nearly ninety years old when she told me: "You have beautiful eyes." My brown Mexican eyes. I had no reply. I wept. She never asked me why, and I couldn't have said. Perhaps on the deepest level, at ten years of age I nearly had to die before she came to realize that in some measure, though I was not much of a stand-in for the iconized Blanche, I was a separate being, her child who had survived, but by then I had become alienated, unable to accept her awakened feelings. Just as I had finally been born to her, I died to her again, another déjà vu of her great lifepain.

Some time before her death I paid her another visit. She was turned out in all her finery, expecting me, propped up under the bed clothes, still in her shoes and stockings. She had turned gentle, a dangerous sign. In the midst of an apparently reasonable conversation, quite suddenly she traveled somewhere else. "That dog will have to be shot," she remarked. I recalled how in her childhood, she had had a Saint Bernard and how, his neck engorged with blood from a neighboring farmer's buckshot, he dragged himself home to die. Perhaps, in some slant way, she was referring to that staying power of hers that wouldn't let her die. But six months later the call came. Two friends rushed me to the airport. By then, she'd waited two days for me. Already comatose, still she raised her skeletal arms to embrace me. I held her hand. Her body gave off the scent of apples.

On the rare occasions when he could afford the trip home, his mother lay there, not saying anything. He remembers her hair, once jet, toward the end become a tangle of stark white, yanked upward from the temples as though she dreamed of horsemen in the night. . . .

The neighbor woman has made her a bed of linen sheets, and she lies there, barely moving, her hands clasped together, empty now of work, warding off the night. She wakes only rarely, her eyelids flutter, her eyes inside their sockets seem not to focus at all, or hardly. Yet, when she opens them, she lifts her arms, thin and transparent as chicken wings, to embrace and cradle him. It is then she begins a kind of song, a rhythmic sighing, as if before she could break the habit of her living, she must shake her life free of all its grief, must pour it out in the soft moans of an ancient child.

He sits by the bedside, touching the transparent parchment of her hands, the veins so thin they must adhere together. Yet she breathes. The lungs do their work, perversely running away with the bit of her life still in their teeth. She is barely sixty.

He thinks he catches the ghost of a smile. But already the bones under the coverlet are curled like a skeleton's, hugging its mouthfuls of earth. Will he ever say of her that she is dead? Or does she carry the seeds of her death, even now, in the pinched, white nostrils that struggle for breath?*

Through the long hours of her dying, sitting at her side, holding her hand, I watched her veins turn dark as bruises. A nurse looked in. "We've never seen anything like this. People usually leave them alone to die."

No sooner had she stopped breathing than the door flew open once more. Another nurse appeared. "Have you called the undertaker?" she asked. "We need the bed."

I waited. In due time, the undertaker showed up. I watched him stuff her stiffening corpse into what looked like a black refuse bag. He loaded it onto a dolly, wheeled it to the elevator, and pushed the call button. I stayed with her body till we reached the curb and the waiting hearse.

> The vehicle pulls away from the curb . . . , a puff of exhaust in its wake. He stands shivering on the pavement watching it, relieved to see it go. . . . The bellhop turns to him almost as an afterthought.
> Wait here, man. I gotta getchu a dolly.
> A dolly?
> Yeah.
> There's no need really. I don't have any bags.
> Regulations, man. We wheel you in here. And when you go, we wheel you out. (*Bardo 99*, Wings Press, 2002)

At the graveside I recited the whirlwind passage from the Book of Job:

> Where were you when the foundation
> of the Earth was laid?

---

* Though Helio, the protagonist of *Face*, is clearly a man of mixed race, his mother's nostrils are white.

> Who took its measure?
> Who stretched the surveyor's line?
> Who laid the cornerstone?
> Who fastened the doors of the sea
> when it burst forth from the womb,
> when I set my bounds upon it and
> clothed it in a blanket of fog, and said:
> here shall thou come and no farther
> and here shall thy proud waves be stayed? (my wording)

I wept for the mother who had known a daughter's love too late, I wept for the daughter who had hardly known a mother.

As if to shed a camouflage, returned to San Francisco I put the theater's inventory on the auction block. It would go to other companies. I passed my 501(c)(3) tax-exempt contribution letter to my late friend and reader, Sydney Carson, director of Nightletter Theater, whose performance work, combining puppets and live actors, although very unlike ours, shared with it a highly dreamlike vision. I cleared desk and life of all distractions. And I cut my hair. Perched in the hairdresser's chair, I watched the long black strands sink to the floor. Perhaps now I could lay my mother's Thessalonians to rest. My theater's publicity had never emphasized my name. If it appeared at all, it kept company with those of our collaborators inside our programs' inner folds. With my mother's death, for the first time, I felt free to claim my work as my own.

13. Writing with the Body

With the demise of my company, I'd lost my community, and having invested a growing sense of identity grounded in my work, its collapse further troubled my sense of self. I touched on these themes in a 1994 interview conducted by scholar and critic Francisco Lomelí, reprinted in the 2013 Wings Press edition of my novel *Face*:

> By putting my theater on the auction block, I was in effect cutting myself off from my artistic community, and by extension, my society. I recognized that I needed to re-invent an identity... before I could forge another community. By the time I began writing *Face*, I had recognized a parallel significance [between] my story and [that of] a man who had suffered a... disfiguring accident... and who elected to perform a radical reconstruction of his own face—a decision which eventually allowed him to rejoin the human race. Stitch-by-stitch as my protagonist reconstructed himself, I tunneled my way back word-by-word into the artistic life [I'd] had to abandon.

I still looked to art as an expression of identity. My former working life had consisted in making theater pieces in collaboration with my company. Whenever I hit an impasse, I developed the habit of arriving early at the studio. I worked out the problem I needed to address alone, on the rehearsal floor, physically putting my body through the state I hoped to evoke. Although tackling a full-length novel was something new, in my subsequent life as a writer of fiction, I continued this habit of *total kinetic recall*, the feeling in my body of striving to imagine the unimaginable. Over time, I put a name to what I was doing. I was writing with the body, much as Latin American women writers Luisa Valenzuela and Clarice Lispector had urged, the natural extension of my work in the theater. I was writing something, something deeply embodied, but on the paper as yet without form. I had an opening salvo to carry me through. But through what?

I had a dawning awareness that in the process of making this new work I was addressing the radical change of my recent life. In a 1981 journal I wrote: "What is this novel about? Mending my face. Redeeming a catastrophe—the loss of my marriage and my source." All those years of risk, all the uncertainty, all the anguish and joy of it, had been preparation for work as a writer of fiction in a transformation as fraught—and as fated—as that of the moth that time, emerging from its chrysalis. But in the writing, although I didn't know it yet, I would begin to unmask myself, to trace the unconscious map of my authentic origins buried deep in my DNA. Perhaps responding to Jean Palmer's suggestion, I would uncover the truth my father had kept from me.

While I wrote, I waged a conscious duel with myself. Who, who was it writing? For some time it had occurred to me that whoever was writing *Face* was not someone hiding behind a departing husband's name. Whoever it was had a different sense of life. *Face* would not be a story of success, or money. It would not inhabit a world of banal certainties and happy endings. Whoever it was was living at the edge, some place where the alleyways turned dusty with human traffic, where people struggled for their daily bread. Whoever was writing was no longer who she thought she was.

Who was she, then? What voice spoke from the scrawled pages of lined paper in the journal, bought secondhand, bound in navy cloth with its repeat pattern of small red flowers. Who?

From my journal: "I want to hit the road. I want to be where my head finds rest at night, not knowing ahead of time where that might be. Find another person each day with whom to share my bread. I want to get to know who I am."

Gradually, despite having lost my community, I discovered the immense relief of no longer having to labor under the pressure of raising funds, of advance booking, wagering on a work's readiness to go before a public. With space to devote the time required to allow ideas to form and ripen. To feel things through. To reject that material which failed to propel the narrative. To inhabit the skin of a protagonist and to sense the things that he—or she—or I—might feel. To make the connections at first not readily apparent. To put inchoate feelings, many of them, to words. To write something (as opposed to writing *about* it) much as I had, in collaboration with my fellow artists, made events in contrast to presenting plays.

From time to time I reverted to "what's next?" anxieties, but words and the shaping of them had settled in my life to stay. They might first spill out garbled on the page, for long, fallow periods they might desert me, but when they were ready, they could be trusted to reappear—if I let them. If I created the conditions to encourage them. If I kept to a discipline of working in those early hours of the morning, when the amnion of dream has not quite yet been ruptured and the unconscious has barely had time to emerge from sleep. Before a public face arranges itself to say "good morning" to the day.

But for the time being at least, fiction would not pay the bills. I managed regularly to book evening performances into the theater space, earning me quite enough extra to meet our needs, mine and my sons', and it seemed right that, rather than letting the theater fall into daytime disuse, I welcomed a young company just starting out to use it. Eiko and Koma, the post-atomic dancers, approached me. They needed rehearsal space; at the time they had no funds for rent. I invited them to use the space free of charge between midnight and 8:00 a.m., when no one else had use of it. Each morning when I arrived at 9:00 to unlock, I found them toweling off.

But when I unlocked the doors one morning, to my utter dismay, I discovered a bare theater, an eerie echo of the *Threesomes* world. The light board vanished; the lights, the risers, the blacks, everything stripped! The means of my support and that of my family had vanished overnight. What was I to do?

Arriving for early rehearsal, the director and the members of his young company, found me in tears. "Never mind," they reassured me, "we'll find your stuff." They rehearsed in many other places. Within days, they had a report. The director of a company renting my space as a performance venue was responsible. When I caught up with him, undaunted by any vestigial bourgeois restraints, I spat out a juicy stream of invective. I marched him to the nearest police precinct, where he sat cooling his heels while I waited for an officer to take a report. Perhaps it helped him that his skin was white. He was given a choice: return my stuff or be arraigned.

Day Eight

In his 2018 article "ICE: The Making of an American Gestapo," Justin Akers Chacón points out how, after 9/11, ICE has become a branch of the U.S. law enforcement apparatus, paralleling increasingly militarized inner-city policing and border militarization. It takes its cue from international U.S. military dominance, and the expansion of its privatization has been a source of both enrichment for a few and exploitation for many, especially migrant laborers, through a process tantamount to criminalization. Under the present administration, federal agents can now deport undocumented people who are convicted of any crime, no matter how minor, such as having a broken taillight, and other issues often determined solely by the agents themselves. And many who are deported are guilty of no crime at all.

But compared to the trials they experience in immigrant detention, what happens to immigrants fleeing the starvation of post-NAFTA rural Mexico or post-democratically-elected-Zelaya Honduras when they reach the no-man's-land of the U.S. border is yet more hallucinatory. These are people who have walked miles through a desert landscape so harsh, seven thousand bodies dead of thirst, starvation, or violence have been discovered over the past two decades with some coroners running out of space to store their remains. In 2018 alone 412 corpses were left to decay in the desert for lack of water and food. Yet from 2012 to 2015, border patrol agents slashed water bottles left for people crossing the desert at least 415 times, and in 2018 nine who dared to leave food or water were prosecuted by the U.S. government for "crimes" and misdemeanors.

I found myself stuck in a limbo job, selling group discount tickets for popular Bay Area entertainments of the kind favored by corporate employees, with no through line to hold onto except the writing—a project without any guarantee. Economic uncertainty weighed on me. I tried my hand at dance and theater reviewing, but the field was narrow to begin with, too crowded to allow any predictability. My internal battle reached a breaking point. One morning I awoke to a feeling as if I had to jump out of my skin, unable to live inside it for another minute. Years later, when the feeling revisited me, I discovered it even had a name: agitated depression. But even had I known it then, I had nothing in my power to tame it.

I remembered hearing of a Buddhist priory somewhere in the Berkeley Hills. I found it in the yellow pages. I signed up for a retreat scheduled from 9:00 a.m. to 4:00 p.m. on one of those fall days when Indian summer makes its last bid before the winter chill sets in. In a skimpy summer getup, I drove to Berkeley, unaware till I parked the car how chill the day had turned. In the *zendo* some twenty-five strangers all sat facing the wall. Tardily I joined them, but no matter how much I studied the graining in the wood paneling, quiet would not come. The room had no heat. I tried gathering myself into a ball. In vain. Ready to toss in the sponge, I waited another minute, and yet another. Finally, on the verge of getting to my feet, I saw the door ease wide, nosed open by a cat. In she padded, heading directly for my lap.

At day's end, we sat drinking lapsang souchong in the *roshi*'s company. Perhaps its exotic flavor made me talkative. Or perhaps it was the *roshi* appraising me. "Any time you need to talk, you're welcome to come over." I shared the story of the cat and how she warmed me. The *roshi* pondered a moment. "She's feeling lost. She used to be the priory's top cat, but two weeks ago we got a new kitten. She's feeling displaced."

Driving back to San Francisco, I took the middle Bay Bridge lane. As the cables shot by my peripheral vision, I kept blinking back tears. Midway I broke down. No way to stop, no windshield wipers to stem the tide. Tough it out, I thought, tears or no tears till you get to the other side.

Why the tears? I wondered. Despite the day's chill, a cat paid my lap a visit, kept me warm, thawed some of the winter in my heart. But back home, with my sons out for the day, the house echoed emptiness. I blew my nose. Sounds of revelers drifted up from Castro Street. It must be Halloween. Five years to the day marking my own displacement with the breakup of my marriage, and, though I had forgotten it, after those five years, my body still remembered.

IV

Getting to the Root of Things

14. Through the Looking Glass

Interspersed between the scribbled crots of *Face*, I catalogued my self-pity. I was still learning to exchange loneliness for the solitude I needed to write. From my journal: "Can I really let all this stuff go, the hopes, the fantasies, cut ... myself loose of my own shadow. Turn truly transparent. What would it feel like then?"

Still at loose ends, supporting my sons by scrounging for work and working part time, at last I fastened on the craft that allowed me to adhere to the tougher discipline that three years of composition required. I took up flower arranging, a paying occupation that yielded creative distraction while allowing me to keep to the stricter stuff of making words.

A year later I was still filling those pages when, journal in hand, I joined a group of friends, four women and one man, in the Mexico City airport to travel with them to the Yucatan. Before heading south, we paid a visit to my cousin Rosendo's Mexico City home, where he welcomed all five of us. After dinner, he brought out a picture of Trinidad Galvan, the grandmother whom as a child I never knew I had. A light-skinned woman, she wore a white lace picture hat in the style of her epoch, a white Gibson-Girl shirtwaist and bustle skirt. She posed for the photographer, resting a dainty white gloved hand on a white lace parasol.

He (or she) was raised by two grandmothers, one a solid citizen, the other a dizzy beauty. One (the redhead) wore black velvet. The other (the brunette) wore frilly white lace froufrous. The redhead had a black velvet ribbon around her neck. The brunette wore a lacy white picture hat. The redhead designed precision chronometers while hatching thirteen children. The brunette regrettably went mad. But Gulen couldn't bring him (or her)self to attend the funeral because he (or she) didn't know which exactly of the two had died, the starchy velvet one who was always squinting through her watchmaker's glass, or the lacy *bonne vivante* who always forgot to arrange for dinner, but who kept foil-wrapped chocolates in her underwear against emergencies. (*Redoubt*, Wings Press, 2004)

Rosendo asked me—hesitantly, I thought—did I want to see my grandfather? He placed in my hands what looked like a high school history book. A photograph showed a lineup of five men. The two to either side wore stovepipe hats. They flanked a short, stocky, bare-headed individual, so short that, no matter how high the hat he might have chosen to wear, still his companions would have dwarfed him. His right hand was jabbed, Napoleon-like, in his vest—a diminutive tyrant, a tyrant with blue eyes!

"He looks like a son of a bitch," I blurted. "How come the blue eyes?"

Because, Rosendo explained, his father was French—something I hadn't known before—an engineer named Teofil Delarbre. Teofil—same as my ex-husband's middle name, the one he never used. When the French were driven from Mexico in 1866, he abandoned his family and returned to France. According to Rosendo, my great-grandmother warned him that were he to leave Mexico, their child—my grandfather—could never bear his name because his birth would never be recorded as legitimate in the Mexico of his day. I remembered my father saying that men who were not loved by their fathers became flawed. But evidently my outburst had touched on something real. My grandfather had been born out of wedlock, Pineda *y que*, and handed down from my great grandmother's generation, my name was matrilineal. Rosendo's revelation came as something of a shock, strong enough to bend my sense of self, but why didn't I have the presence of mind to ask for anything more? Was I settling for an unexamined life, a sort of entry without inspection? I hadn't even asked where my great-grandmother might have come from. What was I still afraid of?

We continued south, making for Puebla, which we reached at nightfall. Not a vacancy. Far distant on the main road, we settled for a truckers' inn. We pressed on, fording desert streams, Oaxaca bound. In San Cristóbal de las Casas, lit by the last rays of sunlight, I sat on a tree stump in a hotel garden run wild, the journal open on my lap. Behind the brambles came the muted sobbing of a very young girl, a man's voice, the sounds of someone carrying her inside, the child still crying softly. I heard the closing door.

> He can hear the sash tearing as he rips open her wrap. He pushes her onto the pile of rumpled bedclothes.... He fumbles with his belt....

Not possible, this rape. To this day, readers of *Face*—some of them—object. Yet wasn't my protagonist made small by poverty's weight? Relentless poverty, the kind found in the favelas of the undeveloped world, generally went unrecorded by the people who live it day after day. But as I wrote, it was my great good fortune to stumble on one exception, Carolina Maria de Jesus' *Child of the Dark*, written by a ragpicker with a second-grade education. In her account of a life lived at the edge of existence, its one moment of relief occurs when she finds a ruined pair of children's shoes in the gutter and watches the expression on her daughter's face as the cobbler repairs what becomes her child's first pair of shoes.

The journal bound in navy cloth with its repeat pattern of small red flowers filled to overflowing. Back home, I shifted to another journal, filling page after page over the three months I spent in the library at San Francisco's University of California Medical Center, attempting to get a grasp on reconstructive surgery. I read extensively, trying to get a feel for grafting skin. Discouraged, I even applied to watch a procedure, but as I knew from my many years of sharing life with a doctor, the practice of medicine is as guarded and sacred as the priesthood. At last, half-hidden in a discard pile, I found one source and only one that truly suited my purposes: *Emergency Procedures in Third World Countries*. Only in this, the most technologically basic branch of medical practice, would I discover what I needed to know. It was in that library I also came across the passage from Maurice Merleau-Ponty in *Phénoménologie de la Perception* that became *Face*'s epigraph: "Like a novel, the face is a web of living meanings, an inter-human event, in which the thing and its expression are inextricably joined."

By the time I reached what I imagined would be the novel's concluding episode, the hunt-to-kill in the coffee orchard, I had filled at least four journals, the many *Face* crots still intercut with dreary complaints about my own sad state of affairs. My companion of the moment offered firearms and ballistic expertise while I shared with him my weary discontents. "You have a choice" was his response. I must have been ready to hear it. I could come to terms at last. Either I could keep grasping to me the pain of loss, or if I chose, I could celebrate its blessings.

I recognized the sea change that had come over me, a change my sons ascribed to my experiment with the munchies. I began to appreciate how Felix had set me free. With a letter to him I hoped to set him free as well: "I want to make sure you know how much I thank you for caring for me during the time I didn't yet know how to put the pieces of my life in better perspective, and for helping to advance the process of setting me free, perhaps a little before, and surely a great deal after I should have been. But I am such a slow learner! Putting it all together has taken me a very long time."

By then, my sons were living on their own. Left alone without a household to look after, I was free at last to turn my attention to the revisions that would see the novel through its final stages. All my work in the theater, all the complexity of working with actors—over time numbering in the hundreds—of collaborating with production colleagues to negotiate the formative aspects of the work, all the coordination with lighting and sound technicians—all those variables had taught me to balance elements, to derive the larger picture from the occasionally rebellious sum of the parts. The ability, before computers, to track in a tangle of sixty to seventy thousand words, to find the words of a particular passage, to determine how and when that phrase might recur, to recognize therein the resonance that lends depth to a narrative and to tap into that unexplained quality evoking the unspoken, to make the unnamed connections lying in the mysterious bed of fiction, that art had become mine. I was free to apportion my time, and my life, as I chose. And without fully realizing it, I was no longer beholden to anyone. I had earned the means to support my habit. From my journal: "I have come to accept that I am alone, able to grow without benefit of a foil. . . . What will it take to remake my face? Will this novel finally show me how?"

Day Nine

The cruel and disrespectful culture of Immigration and Customs Reinforcement has not changed. In 2014 the "rules of engagement" forbade border patrol agents to use pepper spray, Tasers, or batons without having to write a report. They preferred administering beatings with flashlights, which they referred to as "tuning up" migrants and which required no report. Agents were taught that as soon as a migrant picked up a rock, the appropriate response was to "light them up," meaning shoot to kill. There have been recent instances of fatal killings, including the shooting of Claudia Patricia Gómez González, a twenty-year-old Guatemalan woman who was shot at the Texas border in May of 2018.

The Trump administration has made a practice of separating thousands of children, even nursing infants, from their parents, people crossing the border, some of them in search of bettering their economic circumstances, some of them quite legally applying for asylum, fleeing, some of them, from death threats and the terror of seeing close family members assassinated. Whereas in May 2017 there were 2,400 migrant children in detention, fifteen months later there were now 12,800, some of them separated from parents the government has already deported.

The American Civil Liberties Union, suing to reunite a Congolese mother with her incarcerated daughter after four months of separation, found a child in the same facility who had been separated from her family for more than a year! For young children, family separation is particularly traumatic, and its effects will be felt for years to come. For example, recently Swedish researchers have identified more than one hundred children of families facing deportation who have contracted what they call "resignation syndrome," a disorder in which the child withdraws, doesn't react even to painful stimuli, and needs to be fed by feeding tube, sometimes for years thereafter.

On being reunited with his mother, one four-year-old, failing to recognize her, fought off her hugs and crawled into a corner. A five-year-old boy tearfully asked his father "Papi, why did you abandon me?" As of 2019 more than forty people attempting to reunite with their children, people who may be undocumented as well, have been arrested by ICE while trying to reclaim them. And repeatedly authorities "lose track" of thousands of migrant children who have been placed with sponsors, many of them relatives.

A recent 2018 prison strike, which ended on the anniversary of the Attica massacre, held as one of its demands the abolition of slave labor in the U.S. prison system. (The Fourteenth Amendment sanctions it.) Under Obama (deporter of 2 million persons) a former ICE official claims, contractors saved a lot of money by using detainee labor to perform tasks that would otherwise be the responsibility of paid employees. Prison labor, remunerated often by as little as a dollar a day, now under the Trump administration draws not only on adult inmate labor but on child labor as well. A typical day for children held in detention begins with scrubbing toilets. One fourteen-year-old detainee describes caring for an infant in immigrant detention, so neglected she had to feed him and change his diapers. "If I hadn't, no one else would have," she is reported to have said. Some weeks later, the deaths in immigrant detention of Jakelin Caal Maquín, a little seven-year-old Maya child, came to light, followed days later, on Christmas Eve 2018, by the death of eight-year-old Felipe Gómez Alonzo.

15. Facing It

(and a #MeToo Moment Thrown in for Bad Taste)

Face was ready. The final draft was complete. Initially, the manuscript met with some resistance. Wrote one agent, "I do not see how I could successfully place your manuscript with a publisher," while another wrote, "I do think you will have a hard time finding an American publisher for the novel. It reads as if it were a European book, and the introspective aspect of the narrative, together with the... upsetting story behind it, will not easily lend itself to a marketable book." But thanks to letters of introduction provided by novelist Carolyn Doty, whose Squaw Valley workshop I'd once attended, I flew to New York armed with the names of two editors, two literary agents, and four copies of the manuscript tucked away in plain brown envelopes, paranoid that before I could make my drops someone crazed would shove me onto the subway tracks. My thought was that in making personal deliveries, I might make contact with their recipients, but the face-to-face encounters I imagined never happened. I managed to deliver my envelopes to receptionists and in one rare instance to an editorial assistant.

Although I'd survived for the moment, I was about to face the *threesomes* of the New York publishing world, and I was still an innocent. Within a week of my return to San Francisco, Amanda Vaill called. She made an offer to buy *Face* for Viking. I broke out in a full-body rash that very day—the result of a sudden plant allergy. Flower arranging could become a thing of the past now that I no longer needed its creative compensations. Hives or no, my success was a thing of legends. The nail-biting of sixty submissions and fifty-nine rejections wouldn't be my lot. But after two weeks back home, I had to recognize *Face* still wasn't ready. It required a more measured resolution, the denouement that in my ignorance I only knew to call "ending material." Although Amanda Vaill may have thought I was not quite in my right mind, I took the novel back, proposing a six-month delay. It had taken me three years to develop. What difference could another six months make?

In the interim, I sought a literary agent, someone who might represent me in the marketplace where one client's work might be sold to an editor for an astronomical sum while another's could be thrown in—like *Face*—nearly free of charge.* Of my two inquiries, the most prestigious one responded. I showed her my theater portfolio; she shared her feminist perspectives. The deal was struck. She never asked me what I thought the book was worth; had she done so, she would probably have called it a "property." In my naïveté, I would have been at a loss to say.

I meet Amanda Vaill in person. She appraises me quizzically: "Where do you come from?" she wants to know. I try picturing what it is she sees: a woman of a certain age—fiftyish, say—dark hair, brown eyes, black raincoat, boots, a shoulder bag. She must mean, *if you presume to be a writer, why is it I am hearing about you only now?* I'm no Johnny-come-lately, I tell her. I describe something of my years making experimental theater, directing my West Coast company.

Six months later, when I hand my agent the final draft, rather casually she remarks that *Face* will go on to win many prizes. Prizes are the last thing on my mind. I have a godmother panicked that her last days will outlast her savings. Already on my last visit, she's shared with me a recurring dream: "We're at Middlebury for the summer, enrolled in the language program. It's the final day. I line up with my

---

* See Marissa Higgins, "Authors Get Read about Advances, Highlighting Enormous Pay Disparities for Writers of Color," *Daily Kos*, June 9, 2020.

fellow teachers, but when my turn comes to pay the bill, my purse is always empty."

I need to come to her rescue with a novel whose spectacular sales will support her final days in comfort. It comes as a shock when her neighbors call to let me know she's been found nearly unconscious. By the time I reach her side, she's been discharged from the hospital, still very weak. I fail to take in what she says: "Now I'll have to do it all over again."

Sometime later I revisit that time with an excerpt from a story titled "Notes for a Botched Suicide," published in *580 Split*:

"When the time comes," she says, "will you help?"

I hold her hand. "Yes," I say, "Yes, I will help you. I will be there."

"It's very dangerous," she says, "you could go to jail."

Back home, I make inquiries. How many? in what dosage? And I lie. The pills are for me. For my sleepless nights. But the prospect is too terrifying. Anguish overwhelms me. On my way back to visit her in New York, I detour to Israel instead.

Jerusalem. (This is the street Jesus walked.) There's enough here to choke a horse. What if there's too much? What if I cop out . . . ? (Father, father, let this cup pass from me.)

What will I do? Will I sit calmly next to her? Hold her hand? Wait? Wait for the Angel of Death to come? They say it works better if you use a plastic bag. . . .

I find a Palestinian cabbie. "Take me to the tomb of Jehoshephat," I tell him. "Wait for me."

Old stones line the roadway. Behind garden walls, the leaves of ancient olive trees shimmer silver as they have shimmered for a thousand years. The earth is packed hard with centuries of human traffic. The path is white with dust. It drops into the gully. The tombs are carved in the rock. They date back to the first temple. The air is filled with light. There is a faint, paling winter sun. It turns the sweet grass emerald. Shepherds urge their flocks down the path.

"Salaam alaikum," they call to me.

"Alaikum salaam," I reply.

I sit on a rock, dreaming. Where does the spirit go when the spirit flies? Does it fly into the sun? Is it forever suspended in the eternal night of space? Does it hum for a long time afterward? Can it see us? Does it hover still?

The plane from Tel Aviv takes me to New York.

I run. I fly. The heat in New York kills, especially in winter. Radiators that need shutting off. Her commode that needs emptying, the bed to be changed. Groceries to be bought. Laundry to be done. Thieves to be thwarted. Dinner to be cooked. Herself to be washed, dressed, pushed in her wheelchair. Twenty-four hours of it, to be reminded she is loved, not forgotten, not put away on a shelf to die.

"What will happen to me? Maybe we should put me in a home."

"Come on," I say, "that's just what we decided we wouldn't do. You don't belong in a home. You're too independent. A home would surely put an end to you."

"I'll die anyway . . ."

"Yes. But you could have fun dying."

She begins to laugh.

The days pass. I think about it. Very simple. If she asks for them, I'll pass the pills to her. If she doesn't ask, I won't.

I hear her calling from the next room. I am washing up in the kitchen. I turn the water off. I dry my hands.

"What did you say?"

"Did you bring it, the thing I asked you for?"

I walk into the room where she is lying on the couch. "Yes."

"How much?"

"Enough," I say.

"Put them in the drawer. In the little desk," she says.

Nothing more is said. It's our last night. I will return home first thing in the morning. She settles on the couch. Night is falling. I have trouble with the lamp pull. I spread a blanket over her knees before returning to my dinner.

She seems lost in thought. "I lived with peasants once—a whole year. I learned to speak their language. One time, when I was maybe nine or ten, my parents moved to a small village. There was only one school. They were my classmates. And somehow they adopted me. After school, I used to go home with them. They loved me in a way we didn't know about at home. In my family we children addressed our father as "monsieur." I played games with them. They taught me to churn butter, to talk to the cows. There was a way they had of herding them home when it got dark. They were calling them in Latin. She smiles, remembering. "'Quo, quo, ma belle. Quo!'" She grows silent. "The end of a way of life, a more generous way than ours. None of them lived past 50 or so. They died of tuberculosis, all of them. None of them survived."

I sit at her table, contemplating my empty glass, the crusted plate, the linen napkin crumpled on my knees. I am crying—too quietly for her to hear. (From "Notes for a Botched Suicide," published in *580 Split*)

Without quite knowing it, the loss I was mourning is my own.

Six months later, now that *Face* has gone to press, I meet again with Amanda Vaill. Before we leave for lunch she shares a jacket idea—the image of a man, hidden in shadow, dragging an enormous carapace behind him, the pale moon cipher of a face (fig. 15).

I hear my father's distant voice. *Papa Soleil is going to hide behind Mama Moona.*

"Perfect," I say. But do I know exactly why?

To mark the occasion, she's treating me to lunch at an upscale watering hole. We walk down New York's Sixth Avenue in the blinding sunshine of a late autumn day. She wears her customary pearls, her good Republican cloth coat, I, my usual raincoat.

"I think it's wonderful how writers have begun to write about what they don't know," she observes. I offer no reply. What she

FIG. 15. "The image of a man, hidden in shadow, dragging an enormous carapace behind him, the pale, moon cipher of a face." Viking's 1985 cover of *Face*. (Jacket design: Neil Stuart; jacket painting: Christopher Zachow.)

means—she must mean—is how can I, an American woman, in the full privilege of my life—what can I know about living in a favela, days of privation, despair, limitless poverty... know anything about an accident so catastrophic it can send someone's life plummeting into some dark abyss? But do I? *Do I know what the words I've written really mean? What they mean to me?*

The maître d' seats us. "Who are your friends?" Amanda wants to know. She sees my bewilderment. "Writers. People whose work you admire?" It comes to me she's angling for a blurb. "J. M. Coetzee," I say, the author of *Waiting for the Barbarians*. As it happens, I remember he's one of Viking's writers.

"Great! We'll send him a galley," she says, "soon as it's available."

But the story of *Face* galleys is like that of a letter purloined. When the book comes out at last, it sports that same riveting dust jacket, but a bloodless blurb fairly whimpers: "Speaks of interesting things in an interesting way." The anticipated endorsement from J. M. Coetzee hadn't come. I felt disappointment, not so much that his validation might have encouraged readership but that there had been a breakdown in communication. I wanted to share the book with him; if nothing else, he wouldn't have to read a galley. I wrote to him and sent him a copy.

Taking my cue from Kobo Abe, I had intended *Face* to end on a note of indeterminacy—would the protagonist leave the hinterland to return to the capital or would he not? Nothing about "what happened to the girl," but when I meet my six-month deadline, both Amanda Vaill and Stacy Schiff, her then-assistant, plead for more. I'm adamant. *Face* is not a romance, far from it. But back home, I must have rolled out of bed soon after in a somewhat more giving frame of mind because *Face* acquired a more upbeat resolution. There *is* that moment of recognition. Or isn't there? To this day, some readers ask me about the woman: Was it she? Or wasn't it? They look to me to tell them, but my answer never wavers. The novel belongs to its readers now. It's for to them to know.

In quick succession, the prizes came: a Gold Medal from the Commonwealth Club of California, the first time the gold was ever awarded for first fiction; the Kaufman Prize from the American Academy of Arts and Letters; and more recently, as the representative work qualifying its author for a Neustadt Prize, it was nominated for international fiction.

Word came to me that it was up for a National Book Award in the first fiction category. The news swept me away. To add some luster to the occasion, a friend insisted I borrow her fur coat. Why not put on the dog for once? Except when I saw it, her fur reminded me of a mattress. It occurred to me if you're going to whore, you might as well wear a sandwich board.

I flew to New York. In retrospect, I must have read the cards. The first freakish omen came with a room, all expenses paid, at the trusty, musty Algonquin Hotel, hangout of Dorothy Parker and the hallowed Round Table. Room 23 housed a clan of cockroaches prolific enough to populate the Bronx. I beat a hasty retreat, crashing at the cockroach-free home of friends. Still caught up in the whirlwind, the day of the awards I had my hair styled. The results looked like they'd been set in concrete. It needed two showers to wash out, leaving me barely enough time to make the pre-event cocktail hour to honor the elect, agents, publicists, editors of the New York literary scene, and writers like me on the make. Totally ignored and left to my devices, I waited, nail biting in anticipation. Polite laughter gave way to hail-buddy-well-met guffaws. Another half hour passed. Another half hour. The barmen wrung the bottles out of their last drops.

By then I knew: the problem must be *Face*. Through the entryway close to where I stood, Doris Grumbach, one of the three panel judges, stormed in. Massive and infuriated, she glared as she swept past. But the evening had yet to wind down to its conclusion. In the cavernous atrium of the New York Public Library, any announcement of the winners names' could not be heard above the din. By then, I knew mine would not be one of them. *Face* won a face-saving consolation prize. But I hardly cared: my elder son was hugging me. On his way home from his lab in Germany, he'd stopped off to help me celebrate.

Seated upstairs at the after-awards banquet—along with my agent and a now-pacified Doris Grumbach—I wondered why one of the seats at our table stood empty, its place card missing. To my right sat Thomas Sanchez, the number-two panel judge. When I addressed him as *compadre*, he stood up and left.

Midway through the cheese course, the chief judge (number three of the series), whose distinction as the host of America's Longest-Running Game Show catapulted him to celebrity status, ambled over to my table. He deep squatted beside my seat. He just wanted to let me know what a lovely book *Face* really was, how faithful to its characters, how adroitly plotted (it was none of those things). Et cetera.

Et cetera.

Et cetera.

I held every one of my facial muscles taut. I was aware that my interlocutor was holding what amounted to a stress position, torture if it went on long enough. Five minutes? Ten? At last I blinked. "I know what it is," I said. Did I mean the novel? Or was I referring to what must just have happened? By then the age of #MeToo was nearly five thousand years in the making, and I saw no reason to hustle it. Time has taught me that if change is to take place at all, it waits for critical mass. Besides, I'd left my sandwich board downstairs. If anyone there was to make a fuss, it might have been my agent, but she was on dinner break. Only much later would she confirm what I'd intuited long before. According to what Doris Grumbach told her, the award officials had assumed *Face* would be the winner. But Mr. Game Show had nominated his golden boy at large, bypassing all the multiple triaging the award is known for, and he was not about to see him lose. While the cocktail hour stretched to ninety minutes, he'd locked the other two judges in an upstairs room, pressing them to switch their votes. To their credit, they held out nearly a full hour and a half before they knuckled under. Celebrity may have its drawbacks, but persuasiveness is not one of them.

I returned from New York somewhat wiser. On my kitchen table where a friend had left it, a tissue-y blue aerogram from Cape Town awaited me. Carefully typed, John Coetzee had written, "I am deeply impressed by the book, as much by what is not said as by what is said." Of all the good tidings, the accolade I would most treasure had come from him.

16. Summoning the Diamond Boss

Much like Theatre of Man's success with *Murder in the Cathedral* fifteen years before, I imagined once *Face* had been published, that would be the end of it. Until one day a call came from a professor and critic of Mexican American literature. "Are you by any chance a Chicana?" Juan Bruce-Novoa, wanted to know. *A Chicana?* I had never thought of myself in those terms. I knew I couldn't claim the East Los Angeles Vietnam moratorium as part of my history. Even though I'd marched year after year in the Vietnam antiwar protests along with hundreds of thousands, I hesitated to claim an identity that, in the context of the racial phobias of my country, had victimized so many others while leaving me comparatively intact. But when he assured me it had nothing necessarily to do with ethnicity, it simply meant having a father who left his native Mexico to take up living in the United States, then yes, that's what I was. A Chicana. Much later other Chicana writers—sometimes to great success—would join me in the mainstream press, but their narratives bore little resemblance to my own.

Ambivalent feelings about my own beginnings troubled me. I began to wonder if perhaps in *Face* I might find a hidden augury, some message that might point me to those origins. After suffering a catastrophic facial accident, the protagonist of *Face* notices it's left him without a sense of smell; close to the novel's conclusion, as he blows a kerosene lamp out, the smell of the smoking wick eludes him. Smell is linked to the retention of memory. Something has gone missing. What?

He was bending down, examining what he had found. When he heard his father gasp, he did not look up at once. When he saw him, he was sprawled along the row where he had fallen. Someone had cut his throat. Someone with thin shoulder blades that stuck out under his shirt, someone with black, polished leather shoes, disappearing in the softly swaying rows of corn.

Could my words allude to the cataclysmic encounter between the indigenous world of myth, magic, and living in close harmony with Earth, and the European world of rationality and dominion over nature? Certainly on the personal level they emblemized my child's view of my father. When he punishes me it's as if the bad father kills the good father whom I love.

His father says to Helio,

"Why do you squint like that?"
"Because the sunlight hurts my eyes...."
"Put your hand up like this. That's something a man has to know.... Never look directly at the sun."

Face recalls that moment in my childhood, the total eclipse of the sun. The time my father disappeared. I had always considered his act and his explanation of it the summit of cruelty to a child. Had I misunderstood his motives?

Only very recently and quite by accident, in an article about present-day U.S. deportation policies, I discovered that beginning in the 1930s, in an episode of epidemic U.S. xenophobia, this one associated with the financial collapse of Great Depression, the United States deported Mexicans—*nearly two million* of them—from such far-apart locations as Texas, New Mexico, Michigan, and New York! The year 1930 was the year before my father married my mother! It occurred to me that, despite his fabrications, in fact underlying them might be another story, the story of how, when he was still very young—barely a teenager—the Mexican Revolution of 1910 disrupted his life, severing him—and me—from his family and all he had ever known, forcing him to cross the border using someone else's name.

Had I been blind to my father's anguish? All those years he never left home, afraid perhaps of being swept up. Yet could that have ever happened with his advanced degrees and remarkable facility with languages? Unthinkable! But what if he'd felt himself vulnerable? Had he married my mother for her papers? I am horrified to imagine he might have been capable of such shoddiness, the father whom I'd idolized? Yet if 1.8 million were nabbed.... *Some of them from as far away as New York...?*

Why did you disappear like that?

I had to see what you would do.

Wasn't that the name of my childhood fear, that *my parents might disappear?*

> In the street he wears the white handkerchief... has worn it... for how long...? a dark man, hidden, dragging an enormous shell behind him, a white, moon-faced carapace, the cypher of a face....

Racist that he was, could my father have been hiding his own indigenous roots? Had he married my mother for her whiteness? Had he imagined that her papers would guarantee him amnesty? Had he hidden his sexual preference behind a token marriage?

Papa Soleil is going to hide behind Mama Moona.

All this time, I, too... have I, too, been hiding behind a white handkerchief I've inherited?

And my mother, without telling her, had he used her as a human shield? Or had she known? And my own birth...? *Was my birth part of his window dressing?*

There are things you can't understand until you're a little older...

Who was my grandfather?

People owed my father favors.

What sort of man was he? Would the name of someone who practiced law in Mexico City, someone born out of wedlock more than a century ago, someone obscure, appear on the internet, a run-of-the mill lawyer? More than 150 years later?

I found his picture on the World Wide Web, the picture of Rosendo Pineda, my grandfather. There was an article:

> son of Teofil Delarbre, a French engineer and Cornelia Pineda, a Juchiteca....

There he was! And his picture, too. A self-satisfied, diminutive little man, immensely proud... someone of mixed birth. Half Zapotec. Born of Teofil Delarbre, his father's name, as my cousin, Rosendo had once informed me. Mestizo. Which made me... whose birth made me part indigenous! And Cornelia, my full-blood Zapotec great grandmother—their names had been there all along, waiting for me to discover them.

There was more:

> The love of learning and advancement through education has deep roots in this Zapotec community where neither was easy to achieve. One nineteenth century figure who exemplifies the desire to excel in the national arena without abandoning his Zapotec roots is Rosendo Pineda.... Opportunities for schooling beyond the primary level were limited in the Isthmus [of Tehuantepec]. [At the age of fifteen] Pineda had exhausted them when Porfirio Diaz, then President of the Republic, visited Juchitán in the aftermath of the battle of the 5th of September, 1866. As a reward for the support of Juchitán in that battle, Diaz chose six young Juchitecos to be educated.... Pineda was one of the three who went to the Instituto de Ciencias y Artes del Estado in Oaxaca. Under the supervision of Félix Diaz, governor of the state and brother of the president, Pineda completed a law degree. He had already distinguished himself as a poet and an orator, talents that Juchitecos seem to have in abundance....
>
> Pineda was elected Deputado Federal representing Juchitán in the National Assembly..., the first of many positions he was to hold. He became an intimate of Porfirio Diaz. In his brilliant cabinet Pineda was a star, and known as the [Diamond Boss]... and one

FIG. 16. "Pineda was a star, and known as the Diamond Boss." My grandfather, Rosendo Pineda, *El Jefe del Diamante* (*left*); heading the group "Los Cientifícos," which he founded (*center, wearing light suit*), and Mexican President Porfirio Diaz (*right*).

of the few who exerted a balancing force (fig. 16). [The expression derives] from the use in watchmaking of diamond balance wheels [to] provide the most delicate [equilibrium] possible.

Diaz' passionate belief in [reason] is one factor in his desire to remain in power. Despite the fact that he assumed the presidency committed to the notion that there should be no re-election, he stayed in power for thirty years, believing that he and his advisors were the best suited to run the nation on a rational basis....

The basic liberal mentality that has characterized Juchitecos throughout their history gradually left [Pineda] more and more disenchanted with Diaz, who... had abandoned the liberal ideology that had swept him into office in exchange for the power of a dictator. When Diaz asked his advice on the eve of being elected for yet another term, Pineda told him... the best thing he could do would be to decline the nomination. When Diaz fell and Francisco Madero came to power, Pineda was invited to join the maderistas. Though sympathetic to the revolutionary ideology of that party, Pineda refused, remaining loyal to his sense of duty. It exemplifies the kind of independence of thought and action that is so characteristic of Zapotec intellectuals. He died in September, 1914, having seen Madero brutally assassinated in 1913, and his country plunged into an internecine revolution that would pit Mexican against Mexican and... divide his own beloved city. (Anya Peterson Royce, "Ethnicity, Nationalism, and the Role of the Intellectual," in *Ethnicity and the State*, edited by Judith D. Toland)

A deal-maker. A cabinet minister! Recognized in his youth as a poet and orator, a gift that must have leap-frogged a generation—like the monarchs, my favorite butterflies, whose short lives required not less than three generations to make it home through North America back to the Mexican pine forests of the Sierra Madre Oriental—thousands of miles—without any prior knowledge of the forest of their origin.

Juchitán was a community of eight thousand souls when my grandfather was born, but in the present day, it's home to hundreds of Pinedas, not all of them related because, according to Juchitán history, in 1746 one Apolonia Piñeda, a Spanish woman of good intent, adopted thirty Zapotec children and had them baptized, presuming to snatch their indigenous souls from certain damnation in the white man's hell (Anya Peterson-Royce, personal communication). Cornelia, my great-grandmother, was the descendent of one of them. And by the time she was born, the tilde had been dropped.

The story told by Gilberto Orozco in *Tradiciones y Leyendas del Istmo de Tehuantepec* has it that when she met Delarbre she was in the full splendor of her youth, with dark hair, light complexion, a straight nose, curvaceous mouth, and a swinging step, dimples on her cheeks and fire in her hazel eyes. And chances are she was already one of Juchitán's many *commerciantes*, her own person when she took up with Delarbre, and her own person when he left, a poor woman with two sons to raise.

One day not too long ago, as I ironed, Degas' painting *Women Ironing* kept coming to mind: the heavy coal-fired irons, one woman's arm raised as if to brush off sweat. I was on the verge of discovering that, far from being the Spanish heiress my father's fabulations cast her, my Zapotec great-grandmother took in washing to support her two sons, one of them my grandfather.

Did she still hold the river and the trees and mountains sacred—as I have learned to do? Had she still kept her Zapotec name alive? And that unknown woman who visited me once as I lay half-waking, who seemed to bend over me with all the caring of a mother—I wondered if perhaps it was her I'd seen before I fell asleep.

How might knowing what my father kept hidden have changed the trajectory of my life? Would I have found the assurance that might have canceled the self-doubt I've always felt, as if, to a certain extent, I'd been born an orphan? Would I have turned to art to define my life? Impossible to tell. One thing is certain: I would always feel the lifepain of severance from a family and a culture that by rights ought to have been my own.

Once my father described to me what his family's home must have been like. And how his father set up a house where people could stay who had come up from the country to Mexico City to ask him for money to marry a daughter or to educate a son. How sometimes his father invited them to join the immediate family for dinner, but, so as not to embarrass them, the knives and forks were discreetly put away because they joined their guests eating with their hands. Because my father always made it seem like his father was wealthy and had immense land holdings, I imagined these people to have been *peones*, peasants indentured to my grandfather's lands. At last I understood: they were people from Juchitán, my grandfather's fellow villagers, very humble people, come all the way from the south to Mexico City. And how out of deep respect and courtesy, his family reverted to the village custom whenever they came to visit. Here in my northern life it's the absence of this deep courtesy I mourn.

The only stories my father ever told me that had to be entirely truthful were about his wet nurse, a poor Indian woman who slept on the threshold outside his door at night, and about what he ate, "We had pink, fluffy rice and turkey with chocolate sauce." And it occurred to me that there must have been extended family all around him before the family was pulled apart when he was forced to leave Mexico. I remember how he read me a poem once in a language I couldn't understand and how that's the only time I ever heard him weep; it must have been a welling up of his lifepain, the same lifepain I carry with me every day, the great nostalgia of exile I've been carrying all along, an exile reflected in the concluding words of *Bardo99* with its vision of Viek as he's borne on the shoulders of all the people he has ever known: the Africans from Sudan, and the two doctors, Lipsey and Chernoff, from the radiation ward, vomiting all the icons of his childhood, and the cleansing gesture of his mother hanging out the wash to dry, as my great-grandmother must have done.

Viek is still an infant when he dies, not yet fully present to awareness. It's his mother who sings the blessings of earth (in a tongue that hints at Catalan): *tut omens, tut animaes, tut creats, tut ter cant oms, cant ciel e ter, tut cantem gloria,* and I weep for my father because once and once only he showed me his pain. The great pain of exile, of being cut off from everything he'd learned to love. On some level, it is the pain of being born into consciousness, the separation that comes from being born into human life.

Day Ten

One 2019 detainee from El Salvador, crossing the border at McAllen, Texas, reports how detainees were not fed, some of them, for eight days.

Taylor Levy, an immigration attorney working in the El Paso area, wrote a legal declaration:

> I have been working with the asylum-seeking population in the El Paso area for approximately nine years.... I have borne witness to countless stories of rape, torture, and murder. Despite all of this, I have never been as emotionally impacted by anything as intense as I have been working with ... mothers and fathers as they desperately struggle to reunite with their minor children.
>
> On ... June 27, 2018, seven separated mothers arrived at Annunciation House [in El Paso] after having been released by ICE.... These mothers had been told by [Customs and Border Protection] that they were on their way to be reunited with their children. They all believed that their children were already at our shelter waiting for them. When they arrived and realized their children were not there, they were heartbroken. I personally observed the pain and trauma they experienced in that moment.

When I explained the [Office of Refugee Resettlement] process, [one mother] began to sob, shaking uncontrollably. She said she had stayed strong for approximately 30 days away from her child.... [She] was hoping to be reunited with her child that day.... [It] was simply too much for her to take. I spent close to an hour with her before she was able to stop sobbing.

I simply cannot believe that my government could have done this to these people.

I declare under penalty of perjury under the laws of the State of Washington and the U.S.A. that the foregoing is true and correct.

17. Last Things

Over the many months this story came to be, my friend, my colleague in all our years of theater-making, lies dying. Afternoons, I put my work aside and shut the door behind me. I walk the four long blocks to her house. Slowly I mount the steps. Her unlocked door opens to me. Over the weeks and months of her dying, the dog will become so used to me, she will forget to bark. I deposit my things on the coatrack just inside the hall. I walk quietly into the narrow back room where she lies in bed, the special bed, placed there to ease the discomfort of her dying. I move the chair, small enough to wedge between the wall and her bedside, and take my seat. Her dying wish is for me to read to her.

We go back in time, she and I. Sometimes we reminisce how we met. It was a time in my own life when I grasped at the straws of what seemed a dimming future, buried in the collapse of my own theater company. I was trying my hand at theater reviewing, something for which my twelve years as an experimental director had prepared me. And there it was: a small notice, no more than three or four lines in a performance calendar, but they held a promise, something out of the ordinary, visionary perhaps.

Two friends—one of them an actor from my recently defunct troupe—accompany me. Every seat is taken, but a piano bench is reserved for us. The lighting dims. Greased cables crackle in the darkness as an elevator cab slowly rises from below. It hiccoughs to a stop. With a clatter the gate slides open. Under one lone projected light, three lab-coated attendants wheel in a gurney, preparing to autopsy a gigantic fish from which their clamps extract minute pieces of doll furniture.

In a dream state I watch. Later those same pieces will furnish a small dollhouse inhabited by small puppet parents, but by then, I will have fallen into a dreamlike state. Later I will review the performance, scene by scene, remembering its every sequence: the doll furniture, the property of a puppet mother and father keeping house, *marats** both of them, plotting their bad fairy future—echo of my own childhood, of my parents, reduced now to a scary but impotent *grand guignol*.

At the final curtain, my friend comes out to greet us. I'm struck by her vitality, her unruly mane of hair, her flowery hand gestures, and the tomato-soup-red dress covering her generous frame. Much later, I become Nightletter Theater's godmother, passing her the official document, one my late company no longer needs, the 501(c)(3) tax exemption that will allow her company to raise funds; her company's work, though much unlike ours, will keep the mother genes of my own theater's dreams alive.

I am unsure when I began this deathbed watch or when she first suggested I read to her. I ask her if any of the works in my home library might appeal: *Pedro Paramo*, *Waiting for the Barbarians*, *An Unexpected Light*. None of those. She prefers revisiting Bulgakov's *The Master and Margarita*, a book she remembers liking. It's a novel I've never been able to read to its conclusion, but now's not the time to assert my reservations. Although I'm put off by its belabored language, today at her bedside I twist my tongue around its Russian names, otherwise suffocating in its lack of air, its forced humor, its arch rhetoric. After a few days of reading, *poof!* the satanic protago-

---

*A type of puppet operated by the puppeteer with one hand manipulating the head, the other, the puppet's arm, named after Jean-Paul Marat, mastermind of the Reign of Terror during the French Revolution. His unruly physical gestures were said to move at random because none of them came from the heart.

nist appears, his diabolic ectoplasm suddenly manifest, he of the patrician attitudes and cloven hooves, reminder of my father's pointed shoes, his gentlemanly ways.

"Stop," my friend silences me. "Stop. I hadn't remembered Bulgakov. How tedious he is. I'm not loving this one bit."

"Neither am I," I admit, relieved to close the book. We sit in silence. More titles come to mind, books I've been unable to part with. None of them appeals.

"You'll find something," she says.

And I do. In the library of the apartment building where I keep my quarters, the rejects of our reading room pile up. Atop one stack is Maria Dermoût's *The Ten Thousand Things*, a first edition, its dust jacket still intact, a treasure, cast away like so much flotsam by a wannabe librarian. I hug it to me. What better book to read, especially to a dying friend.

I'm late arriving today. I've been writing long into the afternoon. I sit by her bedside. Before I begin, I show her the book. She takes it from my hand, riffles its pages, hands it back. I open to the epigraph: "When the ten thousand things [called living] have been seen in their unity, we return to the beginning and remain where we have always been."

She nods. I keep to my silence, letting her ponder for some time. From the first time I tried approaching it, dying is not a subject I can initiate. Not directly. She makes it clear it's a discussion she's not prepared to have—not yet—at least not with me. She will have her own poignant way of facing it—when the time comes.

I adjust the small unforgiving chair on which I sit, the only one that fits between the wall and bed.

"Get yourself a pillow," she urges, but nowhere is there one small enough to fit.

"I'll bring one with me when I come tomorrow."

"Good," she says. "Now get to work."

So we begin: *On the island in the Moluccas, there were a few gardens left from the great days of spice growing* ... and as I read, time slows to a place and a century far distant, where native peoples, once indentured, were forced to do the white man's bidding, in a landscape whose vestiges still remain three hundred years later, now crumbled by earthquake, on an island populated by a very old lady—the Lady of the Small Garden—and the few servants, trusted and untrusted some of them, who remain as living traces of a bygone time, along with the proas, those double-hulled dugouts whose rare arrivals and departures are still signaled—when someone remembers—by the ringing of what was once the slave bell, its decaying echoes spreading like waves across the waters of the bay.

My friend knows some of this world. A few years back, still vigorous, she joined two friends traveling to Indonesia. The room in which she lies today is empty of decoration, but the porch and the front room are filled with intricately costumed wayang puppets, droll children's toys, demon queen Rangda masks, flying garudas, storyboards—and a husband who cuts himself off from her now she's dying.

Her first and only trip to Asia fired her imagination, although her work continued to rely on junkyard technology—reflected images created by repurposed projectors and mirrors, a curtain of sand lit by high focus light—the stuff of performance art.

At last I come to a stopping point. It's late. "Shall I continue?" I ask her.

"Let's end there for today."

I mark the place in anticipation of our time tomorrow—if there is a time, if she's feeling well enough. I hold her hand. We sit in silence for a while.

I bring a water glass to her lips. She has trouble drinking lying down.

"When I was ten years old and sick with measles, my father had to get me a nursing bottle so I could drink lying down."

"Maybe that's what I need," she laughs.

I take the glass from her and return it to the table at her bedside, a table too small to hold its clutter of skin lotion, prescription bottles, tooth brush and glass, and the small orchid blooming in the glare of her bedside lamp.

"Turn off the light," she says as I take my leave.

My footsteps drag uphill, barely able to return me home, four blocks, three of them uphill. Some days, the way is easier, especially when the setting sun's last rays fire the eastern hills. Other days, each step feels as though it ought to be the last. After some few days of visits, I fix on a favored route, one that takes me past a small family of poplar trees, trees whose crowns emerge from the earth but whose trunks and roots remain hidden by the fence that keeps them from my prying eyes. For a brief time, I pause there, letting myself be transported to the country roads of France, to a time when, with my young husband, those poplar-shaded roads took us adventuring through the country of his birth, a time when we were happy together. In the high branches, leaves tremble in the soft wind of a fading afternoon. New growth flaunts its innocence against the deepening sky. I mark the places where each node has left its tangle of suckers, useful once, abandoned now, marking generations of time passing. I breathe in deep. *Anywhere but here*: the compounds of Asia, of Afghanistan even, their doors kicked in by the thuggish emissaries of a thuggish empire, home still despite its rape, to poplars studding its dusty soils.

I wonder, does this lassitude come from visiting my dying friend —visits that somehow offer me comfort even now—reading to her day after day, or from my grief watching her slow surrender to her final time?

"We never talk about our friendship." I am settling in today, preparing to read to her. I fluff her pillow, help her manipulate the high-tech controls of her electric bed. I unwrap the water bottle I've bought for her, red, plastic and hideous, its sprout retractable as an aardvark's tongue. "Try this," I hand it to her. She drinks, the suction produces a reassuring sound. Satisfied, she hands it back to me.

"When I got so sick with measles, it's my mother who taught me all this bedside stuff."

"She was scared she'd lose you," she observes. She considers. "You're here almost every day. Isn't that unusual?"

What she says is true. Although we've lived in close proximity, months might pass between my visits. Yet, since I moved nearby ten years ago, she's just around the corner—four long blocks isn't very far, not very far at all. The matter of a fifteen-minute walk, maybe twenty if I am tired.

"You're just seeing another side of me, one you haven't seen before." I don't add the obvious: this is not an ordinary time. I say nothing of what I imagine can somehow be recaptured: a time when neighbor looked after neighbor, especially in times of sickness or distress, a time when notions of good form didn't yet apply. But I've learned better than to talk of death, not even obliquely, not since the afternoon I first tried broaching it.

I open the book to where we left off yesterday. We will speak to one another in this way, through the veil of other words, the words of a writer who puts off writing until late in life but who, in the present as she writes, lives in dialogue with her words. Sometimes her allusions are layered, the meaning at first elusive, as she returns to traces she's first laid down in earlier paragraphs, each return etching them in sharper relief: shadow images of three little girls, dead of poisoning five generations back, not to be confused with the three small girls depicted on the lampshade in her dead son's room, the interplay of great and small.

She asks me to reread this passage. I read once more. We stop there for a moment.

"Like Nightletter Theater," I remind her, "your experiments in time and scale," her use of live actors, echoed by small puppet figures, identically clothed so there can be no mistaking, effigies of parents (hers perhaps?), their enormity collapsed, in a performance whose soundscape even now returns me to the night dreams of my childhood *droning on that time buzzing no light or very little. Footsteps. What? Father turning off the light. Rock sleep the dark giving off the smell of me under the bedclothes eyes shut tight hum shapes under the eyelids colored lights shifting changing green and blue against the black.*

We're both born of New York's harsh winters and snow cluttered streets, she from the Bronx, I from Harlem, where apartment doors keep us shut in, our excitements orchestrated by subway trips to the Met's children's chorus rehearsals (hers) or dancing lessons (mine) until each found her way to the theater, where the fear and helplessness of childhood could melt away. Ours has been a thirty-year-long conversation, the way we make our art. She's been my reader for nearly thirty years, always eager to know about my projects, insightful with her feedback.

"How's the book coming?"

"It's trying to tell me something, I can't quite put it all together just yet."

"You'll finish it." The set of her jaw persuades me. "You will."

A team of Filipino women care for her—all of them friends—and do for her what her body no longer can. I know their names and their dispositions: Susan of the round face, and pensive look, and the smells of galangal and lemongrass steaming from her kitchen; Evelyn of the quick step and ready smile; and Julie, old now, her steps halting—she's been doing this work, caring for the dying—for the nearly forty years she's been sending money "home."

Weeks stretch into months. No matter how my friend feels or how more and more her body won't obey, she never yields her dignity. As the days turn warmer and she sheds her nightclothes, she apologizes for lapses she'd never permit herself in life. If she shows any testiness at all, it's with Julie that she's short, Julie who's brought her holy pictures and rosary beads, consolations of the dying. And Julie, distraught now when I find her in the kitchen, where I comfort her, reminding her that sometimes, when people are dying, they're not always at their best. And her sharp intake of breath when she grasps my forbidden word, as if my friend must only just recover from a temporary setback.

But this is leukemia. She used to tell how, when she was a very young woman, some sixty years ago, as a fire-watcher on the California-Nevada border, she watched the sky light up with each detonation of a test explosion. Highly likely some stray nanoparticle of radiation, innocently entering her lungs, first announced its devastation.

Outside, as the spring advances, there's a blazing sun; inside she lies in obscurity, staring at blank walls. When I read to her, it's by the light of her bedside lamp. How would she feel today if I opened the garden door? Would she like me to pull the heavy velvet drapes aside and let the sunlight in?

"That's better," she sighs deeply.

Now, from where she lies, she can hear the sound of water burbling in the fountain and watch the sunlight strike the hanging fern outside as it rotates this way and that, propelled by a gentle breeze.

"What's the news of the outside world?" she asks me.

I don't tell her of immigrant raids, the separation of families— how can I?—terrified people living in the shadows, the death of a tiny Maya girl migrating north with her dad, thrilled about walking 2,500 miles in her first pair of shoes.

"Remember when I told you if I had it to do over again, I'd want to come back indigenous?"

"You found you are?"

"I even found my great-grandmother's name!"

She laughs. "Now you don't even have to come back!"

Today the French doors are open. "How about some water before we start?" I pass her the plastic bottle. She shows some confusion as to how its spigot operates. I sit by her bedside, riffling the pages, finding my place. We hear the door opening. I recognize her daughter's voice coming from the front room, where her dad stays apart. Quite suddenly she's at my side, beaming down at me, happy that someone is breaking up the days her mom has to lie alone with her thoughts. She fusses over her, fluffing the pillows, adjusting the bedclothes, making sure she's comfortable.

It comes to me that with this reading it's not just my friend's passing that I'm easing, but family and caregivers, too, whose smiles greet me as I arrive, who tend to want to delay my leaving, tempting me with soup—just a taste?—or telling me how my friend is getting on. They, too, feel this passage keenly.

I phone to tell her I'll be late today. "I don't know how you'll find me," she speaks to me from her land line. "I don't know where they've taken me. I don't know anyone here."

When I arrive some time later, she asks me if my journey's been a long one.

"Four blocks," I answer.

"How did you get here?"

"I walked—but I took my time." A *lifetime*, I'm inclined to think.

She's mystified. "I don't know where I am. Everything here looks the same, all the doorways, the windows, the wood trim, but I don't know what they're doing here."

I listen quietly.

"The coved ceiling, the moldings, all the things I love. Evelyn says they came to be with me because they love me. But I don't know how they got here."

"How do you feel about that?"

"It's disconcerting." After some time she adds, "There's no explanation."

"And Nightletter Theater, how did you go about all those years of image-making?"

"There's no explanation."

"Maybe that's a good thing," I say. "Maybe, sometimes when there's no explanation, it opens the doors of poetry."

She reaches an emaciated hand—her once-beautiful hand—to touch my face.

"You're the only one who doesn't want to correct me," she says.

It's Friday, the eleventh of August, night of the new moon. I attend a demonstration at ICE headquarters in downtown San Francisco, brandishing my sign that shows eight iconic silhouettes of children who've died in detention. "How Many More B 4 We Close the Camps?" But battling the winds gusting along Sansome Street, it's all I can do to hold on to it.

Back in the East Bay, exhausted, sitting at the bus stop, I debate my promise to look in on my friend today. I strike a bargain with myself: if the No. 18 is first to come, it will detour me to her house, if it's the No. 6, I'll go home for the day. The No. 6 arrives. I am not with her family gathered at her bedside.

It is the day she dies.

Sometimes it hits me, all the things I want to tell her the day we were together for the last time, the day before I took the No. 6.

I'm quiet, holding her hand, sitting on the small, unforgiving chair, wedged tight between wall and bed, so tight my knees don't always have the room they need to feel like knees.

"I love all these things. All of them," she says. "When I'm lying here alone, I look around, at these windows, at these cornices, at these walls and ceilings.

"And I ask myself, how did I get here anyway?"

ACKNOWLEDGMENTS

Books, mine at least, hold something in common with movies. Whenever I watch those credits roll, I am reminded of all the conversations and the support lent me by so many. By my colleagues, Professors María DeGuzmán, Marissa López, Francisco Lomelí, Elizabeth Willis, Stefania Pandolfo, Marcus Embry, and most especially Marcial González, who read the manuscript (when the working title was still *Waking*) during the time he had to read 140 professional job applications as well. Such amazing generosity is deeply appreciated.

I thank my late friend Sydney Carson for a lifetime of encouragement, and Jeff Biggers, Ann Smith, my colleague in theater, and Ann Vermel, my college classmate, for their helpful remarks, and my longtime friend and colleague Maria Gilardin. I thank my friend Fred Curchack, with whom long ago I shared some precious theater days, for a lifetime of encouragement and support. I thank Elizabeth Fuller for a lifelong conversation sharpening our perceptions and our art. I thank my longtime "daughter-in-art," Shelley Hirsch, for her help and generosity over a lifetime of making art. I thank Jean Crossman, whose life-in-art paralleled mine so many of our years together, and Leslie Abel of the *Murder in the Cathedral* cast, Tim Noakes of the Special Collections Library at Stanford, and Kari Treese, editor of *580 Split*, and my patient editor at University of Georgia Press, Jon Davies. And I thank J. M. Coetzee, whose encouragement has spurred me on from the time *Face* first appeared.

I thank my Mexican cousins, Ana Pineda, the late Rosendo Pineda and his son Rosendo, Ricardo Jaramillo, and Stephanie de la Torre Cataneo, for keeping me in contact with a branch of my family that couldn't quite be severed.

I thank all my friends who had to listen to my *longueurs* day after day as I tracked my progress over the past three years, Steve Zimmerman and Roger Herried and so many others. And above all, I thank my son, Michael Leneman, without whom *Entry Without Inspection* could not have been completed.

The process of self-discovery is a long and arduous one.

APPENDIX

Jean Blum: Finger in Goliath's Eye

PART I

Published in *La Bloga*, April 24, 2010

> To be hopeful is not just foolishly romantic. It is based on the fact that human history is a history not only of cruelty, but also of compassion, sacrifice, courage, and kindness.
>
> What we choose to emphasize in this complex history will determine our lives. If we see only the worst, it destroys our capacity to do something. If we remember those times and places—and there are so many—where people have behaved magnificently, this gives us the energy to act and at least the possibility of sending this spinning top of a world in a different direction... And if we do act, in however small a way, we don't have to wait for some grand utopian future. The future is an infinite succession of presents and to live now as we think human beings should live, in defiance of all that is bad around us, is itself a marvelous victory.
>
> —HOWARD ZINN

Her hands working constantly, Jean Blum loops yarn over the pins of her knitting bobbin; the spool pays out the makings of a fashionable red scarf. Behind her as she talks, a conservatory of exotic plants catches the sunlight, bouncing it off an abstract painting on the wall. Jean Blum is a short woman, standing barely five feet tall, with a sharp mind, given to rich imaginings.

A news photo, taken against a backdrop of the Monmouth County Correctional Institution in an article by Nina Bernstein of the *New York Times*, dated April 3, 2009, shows a forlorn looking woman, a woman identified as a Holocaust survivor, founder of an immigrant detainee advocacy organization American Liberty and Freedom for All, or ALAFFA.

On a first viewing, I wondered who she was. What drove her to engage for many months in such discouraging and thankless work? Was it her memories of her World War II experiences as a displaced person? Had those memories been put aside as she lived an early life described in the article as closely modeled on the American Dream? Did love have anything to do with it?

"When I was maybe six years old, my mother warned me, 'you have to go away for a while, but you must never forget that you are a Jewish child. You must remember not to tell anyone, because if you do, terrible things will happen to you and to your parents.'" Jean Blum pauses to unravel the tangling red scarf before continuing with our interview.

"The next day my teacher—one of the unsung heroes of the French Resistance—spirited me away to a convent where I lived with other girls whom I discovered much later were also Jewish." When Blum's mother came to take her back, Blum failed to recognize her—"I never thought I would ever see her again," she explains—but the gravity of her mother's admonition never left her.

Now seventy-three, Blum was born in Warsaw, an only child whose father was an electrical engineer. The Polish government charged him and an engineering colleague with designing and overseeing the installation of the telephone and telegraph communication system. The first week of September 1939, immediately after the first German bombs fell on Warsaw, her father received a phone call in the middle of the night from the Office of the President of Poland ordering him and his electrical engineering colleague to show up at the bus depot at 6:00 a.m. with their wives, their children and one suitcase for each family. They were allowed to escape, not because the Poles were particularly concerned for the family as endangered

Jews, but because her father possessed the information they needed to deactivate the system he and his colleague had designed so that it would not fall into German hands.

After conducting them to Romania, where they debriefed the two engineers, they left them to shift for themselves. Stranded in Romania, Jean's father began making the rounds of all the embassies in Bucharest searching for a country willing to take them—to no avail. Finally, through their embassy, the French government made him a deal: if he agreed to join the French forces, Jean and her mother would be permitted to travel to Nice, where they would be allowed to stay throughout the duration of the war. Her father, however, would fight with the French. But after the fall of the collaborationist Vichy government he was captured by the Germans. He was sent to a prisoner-of-war camp, and as a prisoner of war he escaped the almost certain extermination that awaited most European Jews in the death camps.

"The Germans treated him better than Immigration and Customs Enforcement treats our American Immigrant Detainees here in the U.S.," says Jean Blum. "My father loved America; he believed in America because this was the only country that would take us in at war's end. I am glad he didn't live to see what's happening now."

Although American public attention is still focused on the horrors of Guantanamo and Abu Ghraib, the existence of a growing number of domestic immigrant detention centers still largely remains under the radar. There are now more than three hundred, located throughout the United States, some federally run jails, some county facilities, some run by such private operators as Corrections Corporation of America and Wackenhut, now doing business under the sanitized name of the GEO Group. They house a total of more than four hundred thousand persons, almost all of them immigrants and with few exceptions people of color. Before the elections of 2008, these institutions were subject to little or no government oversight, and even now under the aegis of Department of Homeland Security (DHS) Secretary Janet Napolitano, the new administration is not showing signs of producing much in the way of change.

Blum remembers the limbo state that people displaced by World War II experienced. When at war's end her mother and father were reunited, no country was willing to take the family in until, through the intercession of her father's brother, Sholem Asch, the family was permitted to enter the United States by way of a special act of Congress. Used to a prewar life of relative comfort, they found themselves living on the fifth floor of a roach-infested Bronx walkup apartment. Her father repeatedly had to scramble for work, first as the employee of a brother who owned a record company. Her mother found work as a fabric picker. Left at home alone, and overwhelmed by the adjustment to a new school where she spoke no English, Jean cried incessantly. One day her father came across Margaret Bourke-White's photographs of the concentration camps taken at the time of the liberation. He carefully cut them out of *Life* magazine and taped them to the walls of Jean's bedroom. "These are the people who have something to cry about," he told her; "nothing happened to you."

"We Fear for Our Lives"

The pictures of World War II concentration camp survivors remained on Jean's wall for a limited period of time, but they never left her imagination. When Blum first discovered that there was a New Jersey–based advocacy organization, the New Jersey Civil Rights Defense Committee (NJCRDC), that tracked incarcerated detainees, she was quick to join.

Shortly before the Memorial Day Weekend in 2005, NJCRDC fielded a call on its hotline from an inmate reporting that there had been a violent incident at the Passaic County Jail in Paterson, where a number of detainees were being held. But with the holiday approaching, there was no one available to investigate. True to form, Blum stepped up to the plate. "I had a habit of volunteering when I saw a need," she says, "and from that moment, I was hooked." Her first report, running to four pages, documents the statements of four detainees who described being repeatedly roughed up, beaten, seriously injured, and verbally abused by guards.

"This [summary] of the events of May 26 . . . starting at 8:20 P.M. [combines] information from Luis Ortiz, Willy Hernandez, and Nguyen Vu. [Vu] had asked another inmate to have his girlfriend mail him a musical birthday card that he wanted to send to his wife. When . . . Corporal C. Jimenez handed out the mail, she . . . wanted to remove the musical portion of the card. Nguyen . . . asked her to leave [it] on because he was sending it to his wife. Corporal Jimenez yelled, 'No, I can't do that. This card does not belong to you.' He replied . . . 'no, this card belongs to me.' She continued yelling . . . that she would call the Sergeant or the Captain. . . .' He answered 'I don't care who you call over because this card is mine.'

"A few minutes later Sergeant J. Arturi came in, plus 'about 5 or 10' other officers. . . . They told the prisoners to face the bars, aiming chemical spray inches from their faces. All the . . . reports agree: 'they grabbed Nguyen Vu by the arm and the neck. He was pushed, shoved, slapped, punched down the hallway in sight of . . . two units returning from recreation, until they got him down the hall where they closed the door so the others could not see.' Nguyen states 2 video cameras taped what happened there.

"The sergeant . . . slammed his head into the wall where it started to bleed. [Vu] felt dizzy. [Three or more officers] 'pushed me to the ground, started punching me, pulled me up, handcuffed me and took me to the Medical Unit.' He was 'so upset and scared' that all he wanted was to be left alone and [he] refused medication. Then they . . . strip searched him . . . and threw him into the hole. . . . [In all] he requested meds or a doctor four times over four days, to no avail. The next day two officers took him to a hearing, telling him he was charged with Attempt to Assault. He was found innocent and the case was dismissed. . . .

"[The inmates who observed the initial beating] 'yelled, protested, banged on the tables. . . .' While this was going on, Hernandez 'fixed his pants.' Officers yelled he had a weapon in his sock that he was trying to place in his shoe. He was 'yanked by his neck, arm and shirt over the edge of the table. He was slapped on his neck . . . and on his back. . . . They continued to slap . . . and rough him up. They kept inquiring about a weapon, but it didn't exist.' Hernandez states: 'They also raised the camera,' (meaning they did not tape this incident)."

Blum's report concludes with the statement of a fourth inmate, Luiz Ortiz, that for now they would suspend their hunger strike "because we fear for our lives."

Administrative Detention: (Il)legal Stranglehold

But Blum soon became dissatisfied with the emphasis placed by the NJCRDC on freeing all immigrant detainees based on the unconstitutionality of holding them without charge. She resigned to found ALAFFA because she preferred to concentrate her efforts on the more immediate task of helping the detainees directly, and believed she would be more effective intervening at the local level. Through an umbrella organization, she obtained tax exempt status, but her efforts to secure funds to support her activities and to expand her operation were largely unsuccessful. She continued on her own, very much as a one-person operation, occasionally supported by the help of volunteers like herself.

An excerpt from an early ALAFFA newsletter dated November 26, 2005, speaks volumes about Blum's sense of mission:

A.L.A.F.F.A. cares a lot about what is happening to you.

- We don't want to see people maltreated, separated from their families, be denied justice and compassion.
- We care about you because you are our neighbors, our friends, our family.
- We know that if they can do this to you today, they can do it to us tomorrow.
- We are ashamed about the disgrace to our country and the violation of our laws.

From the time Blum's name and coordinates first became known to the prison grapevine, she began to field collect calls from detainees incarcerated in the Passaic County Jail. Besides visiting, she wrote letters on their behalf, helped them file official complaints, made contact with their families and lawyers when the jail phone lines remained blocked for long periods of time, made sure to obtain signed releases from each one of them allowing their stories to be made public, and, although she is a retiree living on the uncertain bounty of a fixed income, she gave them money, and helped them obtain food and clothing when they were released. "They called me only for legitimate problems. They never complained. In fact, I remember one conversation I had with a Nigerian to whom I observed that conditions there were abysmal. His reply was: 'Jean, it is better than so many other places on earth.'"

Although immigrant detainees are arrested and held by Immigration and Customs Enforcement (ICE) under the aegis of the Department of Homeland Security, it is important to understand the place they occupy within the present U.S. justice system. They are not criminals. In fact, "these are people who work hard, many of them heads of families, trying to better themselves, striving for the piece of the American dream, as all of us did," insists Blum, but she points out that many of them will be deported anyway for past misdemeanors such as having a broken taillight or not paying tax on a packet of cigarettes because they are being held in "administrative detention," a provision of the Illegal Immigrant and Immigrant Responsibility (IIRIRA) Act of 1996 which, under Title III, denies them the right of appeal such that they can be removed without judicial oversight.

Whereas under the Constitution, not only citizens but all persons are accorded the right to defend themselves before a court of law, under the provisions of "administrative detention" an entire group of people—mostly poor and almost all persons of color—has been denied that right. In fact, although mostly staffed by Caucasians, the detention system holds persons primarily from Central and South American countries, the Caribbean, Africa, and the Middle and Far East. "The entire ICE operation is in violation of the U.S. Constitution," Blum points out, "so they excuse it by saying that [the Constitution] only applies to U.S. citizens—yeah, like being a little bit pregnant." Not only does "administrative detention" establish and perpetuate a dangerous parallel, unconstitutional system of punishment, but once the law is compromised, it may be used to apply to any other demographic group.

PART II

Archive of the Detained

Published in *La Bloga*, April 27, 2010

Over the many months Jean Blum worked directly with the immigrant detainees, she kept files of their letters and their complaints, as well as background materials, as news of detainee abuse began to make headlines. Her archive, which she made available to me over the course of our ten-day interview, includes documents from the Department of Homeland Security, official "incident" reports, complaint forms filed with the Passaic County Jail administration, and letters written to her and to others by detainees, some attesting to conditions still now unimagined and unknown to most Americans. The sampling below only begins to describe the kind of conditions the detainees were enduring then and that more than four hundred thousand of them are still now forced to endure.

Infrastructure at Passaic County Jail during the time Jean Blum was intervening on behalf of immigrant detainees being held there is described in a December 12, 2005, affidavit filed by Shayana Kadidal, Esq., of the Center for Constitutional Rights, who refers to it as "an aging, decrepit facility with very poor conditions.... The roof in the main immigration detention ward was leaking, causing a greenish growth and black mold to cover the entire ceiling, which would then drip and fall into detainees' beds [and] food."

Diet is inappropriate and inadequate not only at Passaic but elsewhere within the detention system. In a summary of grievances dated January 16, 2006, detainees at New Jersey's Monmouth County Correctional Institution (MCCI) state: "The portion of the food is barely enough for an adult. The portion is very small and the quality is very bad. (Every day all three meals, 'potatoes', and a lot of cold cuts a week). The food also is cold most of the time, which is not the quality of standards in the DHS/ICE rulebook stating: 'one cold meal and two hot meals a day.' Most of the time, all three meals are very cold. We believe that the jail is "racketeering... to force us to purchase their food from commissary, so the jail would be able to collect their 10 percent profit." A specific dinner menu is described "8 to 10 oz. of rice with 20 to 30 red beans added and 4 tablespoons of wilted [lettuce.]"

In the early months of 2006, during the period when immigrant detainees were being exchanged for U.S. Marshal prisoners, extreme overcrowding was the order of the day. A February 28, 2006, letter to Blum from newly arrived detainee Luis del Orbe states: "[When I arrived at] the Passaic County Jail... I was held in two separate holding cells at different [times] until I was issued a sleeping mat and placed in a dormitory at 9:35 p.m.... At all times these cells are at nearly [three] times over their maximum capacity.... I was escorted to a basement dormitory.... This dormitory has forty-eight sleeping bunks, yet eighty-nine individuals are expected to sleep there. Through the four days and three nights I was there, the number of individuals increased as more of the recently arrested [were] brought in. Those who are unable to sleep in a bed are given plastic mat containers, which are placed at any available space on the floor. Those who did not get these plastic mat containers must place their mats in any available floor space...; anyone needing to use the toilet facilities must... hurdle over those individuals sleeping on the floor.

"While sleeping on the floor... one of the individuals going through his drug... withdrawals vomited on me. Since there was no hot water available, I had to take a cold shower and be given new jail clothing.... Due to the poor ventilation... there was at all [times] a temperature above 90 degrees.... [C]onditions... were not made any better when the K-9 unit being handled by Corporal Mercado defecated on the floor of the dormitory, a space [it] just so [happened] is at face level where I was sleeping on the floor." Blum describes how detainees were so overcrowded they could not all sit down at meals and how some were forced to sleep on tables. She identifies leakage problems from bathrooms and in walls as causing further crowding of detainees.

Inappropriate mingling of inmates was frequent. On August 26, 2005, Xiomara Guity, in a report that asked, "If you feel that you have been physically or sexually abused or your conditions of confinement have been abusive, please explain below," responds, "I had to go to court. To go and come back from court they put me in the back with the guys. It was about 6 guys to just myself. A guy that was getting sent to Barbados said: 'Damn, I haven't been this close to a girl in over 5 years.' For the strip search, they do it [in] front of everybody, in front of inmates, officers. Couple weeks ago, a male sergeant saw the girl half-naked." In an undated letter, Ruth Jean-Baptiste writes: "Strip search is very [humiliating]. The fact is that we are from a different background, the strip search in public hurts a great deal." And an anonymous November 13, 2005, SOS scrawled on a napkin reads: "Transportation to court (men and women together) very frightening."

Incoming and outgoing mail privileges, and telephone access are critical to insuring the civil rights of immigrant detainees. Blum shares a letter of June 17, 2005, from Lee Ngai addressed to her regarding his "mail which I haven't received in two weeks. My family is in the process of backchecking my mail to see if it arrived at the jail. My problem [concerns] my legal case. My lawyer mailed in documents [stopping] my INS [Immigration and Naturalization Service] appeal on 12/2/04. My family called to see if the documents arrived and they did.

"My INS appeal was [stopped] and I have a receipt for it [but] I didn't receive my 90 day review. My [family] was told that something was wrong with my file. My D.P.O. [Deportation Proceedings Officer] wasn't notified of my immigration appeal [stoppage] and date.... My lawyer called the court that he mailed the documents. They told [him] they forgot to date the documents.... Two weeks later I found out the date they put on my documents was for May 26, 2005. After six months [are over] if the INS do not deport you, they are [supposed] to let you go. But they started my 6 months [all] over [again], and took [away] the six months I already did.... Do you think it's possible for me to get my six months back?"

In a report dated January 16, 2006, from the Monmouth County detainees, "Our mail is coming in late a lot of times, or being returned for no reasons at all. It does not state why it was returned. There were several detainees, that when their families sent them a money order, [it] was returned to the sender because it had M.C.C.I. on the envelope.... Also the prison is violating our rights by opening all our legal mail. The envelope states, 'Legal Mail.' They would just ignore it and open it without our consent. All legal mail, by law, is to be opened in the presence of the addressed person.... Most of the time the mail is either ripped or sliced in half before we even receive it."

Detainees were unable to make outgoing phone calls either to families or to their lawyers—those few able to afford lawyers—for extended periods of time because the phones were frequently blocked, or the access numbers changed. But when the phones worked, detainees were obliged to purchase phone cards from the prison administration costing ten dollars for the first five minutes and eighty-nine cents for each minute thereafter. A request to ICE dated August 15, 2005, signed by twenty-eight detainees reads: "We would like to know why our phone service [is] blocked. We have to get in touch with our families, lawyers, business associates, etc.... Can you please get this block removed?"

A Guyanese detainee complains, "On August 1, 2005 the jail have changed their telephone company to a company called (Global Tel Link). Since the phone company has changed, all my attorneys' phone numbers have been collect-call blocked by the jail-contracted telephone company. [It] is [illegal] to block legal phone calls to attorneys and legal representatives. The jail-contracted telephone company requires each individual [attorney] to set up an account before the detainee would be able to place a collect call to their legal representative."

A press release from the Washington chapter of the National Lawyers' Guild dated January 25, 2007, quotes detainee Rafiu Abimbola: "I was detained for six years. The telephones frequently did not work and legal materials were unavailable or out of date. Because I was managing my case on my own, this was extremely hard for me. DHS did not attempt to fix these problems. When I complained to the jail, I never received a response and sometimes was punished for complaining. There are no consequences to the government for failing to obey its own standards." Despite his ongoing appeals, Mr. Abimbola was deported to Nigeria.

In a letter dated October 27, 2005, Heung Wah Wong, who was

eventually transferred to Oakdale, Louisiana, asks Blum to address a letter on his behalf to the Fifth Circuit Court subject lined "Petition for Review of his detention that commenced in 1997 at F.D.C. Oakdale, Louisiana.... His proposed draft reads, 'Mr. Wong has on several occasions written and [requested] that ICE transfer him back to Louisiana, but was constantly rejected.... Mr. Wong's detention at Passaic County Jail is very repressive. He's confined 23 hours a day [in] lock-down and is unable at all to research his case in the law library because it is insufficient [time] and only allowed 1 1/2 hours twice a week to use the law library.... Transferring Mr. Wong back to Oakdale, then he can be able to exhaust his administrative remedies.... P.S. The only reason Mr. Wong is held at Passaic County Jail is because ICE has a contract lease with the jail [although] his case was in the southern district.'"

In blog "The Business of Detention: Cracking Down on Immigration and Locking Up Profits," Renee Feltz and Stokely Baksh describe conducting on-site visits to twenty-three detention facilities. They write, "at 12 of the 23 facilities visited, the number of the OIG [Office of the Inspector General] was blocked. When [detainees] called the complaint line, they would get a voice prompt that "this is an invalid number," or "a call to this number has been blocked by the telephone service provider.... At Corrections Corporation of America's Elizabeth Detention Facility, a privately owned and run jail in New Jersey, the list of consulate numbers was six years old. When auditors called 30 of the consulate numbers on the posted listing, they found that 9 were incorrect."

Frequently inmates' legitimate phone requests are met with punitive consequences. Egyptian detainee Osama Metwalvy's letter of December 14, 2005, states: "I just come to Passaic County Jail. I asked officer if I can make phone call to let my family know where I am. He said 'No. . . .' I show him the Book for Rule [The Inmate Handbook]. He said 'fuck the book. We here don't use that.'" When Metwalvy appeals to the ombudsman, "he told me 'fuck you, you mother fucker.' I get so, so upset. He told me . . . 'I will call the sergeant.' [Later] the same ombudsman [jumped] on me and two [officers surrounded] me on the floor and he start beating and punishing me . . . Another C.O.

came and spray me with O.C. [pepper spray] in my eyes... 5 or 6 officer was beating me. After that they... put me in the box for 30 days. They told me 'next time we will kill you!'"

A memorandum of December 14, 2005, signed by thirteen detainee witnesses corroborates Metwalvy's account: "We... saw five officers pinning down and holding a detainee. They were punching and kicking him while he was handcuffed. We heard the inmate screaming that he was not resisting the officers and the officers still continued to hold him down and hit him. Sergeant Washington used pepper spray. After... they carried him away to another unit." Luis Ortiz, in a July 3, 2005, memo addressed to Deputy Warden Bendl, states: "Please respect our human rights. All we ask from you is to be treated like human beings. Verbal abuse is not part of the ombudsman job. We are not creating any trouble for you. DHS placed us here, and they may want you to meet federal guidelines. Happy 4th of July!"

Civil rights of detainees were repeatedly violated. Often as a punitive measure, detainees were placed with the general jail population. Their right to special food, halal or kosher, was repeatedly ignored. Often their dietary complaints resulted in their being placed in the hole. Two complaints by Sami Al-Shahin of August 2005 allege profound disrespect for the Holy Quran. "In the past week we have had two shakedowns and in both... the officers have thrown the Holy Quran on the floor.... Officers have to understand the Rules of the Quran. They or anyone can't touch [it].... Maybe this is strange to them but this is our religion.... If this happens again we will have a complaint in the court. Some of us don't have any criminal records so we don't deserve this treatment. If we don't get an answer we will hunger strike for death." In a letter to Blum dated July 17, 2005, Raed Alanbuke writes: "I got my [prayer] beads back, but the rug I didn't get. The Deputy Warden, Mr. Bendl said, 'they are not allowing prayer rugs at this time.'"

Raed Alanbuke's is an interesting case. Together with his brother he was held for over seven months although neither was guilty of any infraction. But they were sons of the UN Deputy Permanent Representative of Iraq. The U.S. government detained them in an effort to put pressure on their father to defect. He refused. In the same letter, Alanbuke writes, "my case is not only about an innocent person in jail, no, it's so much more than that, it's about Iraq, about WMD, about the Bush administration intent to invade Iraq before 9/11/2001; it's about forcing a high ranking [UN] Iraqi diplomat to defect, and when he said 'no,' they waged a war against him."

It is not uncommon to observe that Muslims receive exceptional treatment at the hands of jail personnel. In his affidavit of December 12, 2005, Shayana Kadidal, Esq., states: "Muslim male immigration detainees of South Asian or Arab descent were... systematically denied access to attorneys, phone calls, and bond. The... detainees were frequently detained for months after their final deportation orders for the purposes of criminal investigation. They were also repeatedly and unnecessarily strip-searched; one of our clients... despite being held in solitary confinement was strip- and cavity-searched before entering an immigration judge's courtroom, and, absurdly, also strip- and cavity-searched upon leaving that same courtroom. Dogs were systematically used to intimidate Muslim detainees, especially at the Passaic... facility where many were held. Both the use of dogs and the systematic use of nudity as a humiliation tactic... mirrored... tactics used at Abu Ghraib and Guantanamo."

Blum's archive of Passaic County Jail abuses includes documentation of the use of dogs to terrorize detainees even dating back to before her active involvement there, including a case involving Mexican detainee Rosendo Lewis-Oropeza, in the words of the abusing officer himself. In an incident report by the Passaic County Sheriff's Department dated May 10, 2004, Captain J. De Franco states: "I grabbed the front of the inmate's shirt with both hands and pulled him to the ground. The inmate started kicking and swinging his arms. At this point the inmate attempted to get up when K-9 Officer Tangorra stepped in with his K-9. The K-9 bit the inmate on his left forearm." However, in the same report, the examining nurse, a Jocelyn Cruz, describes both a wound in the left arm and another open wound on Mr. Lewis-Oropeza's left thigh.

There are countless witness reports of inadequate or nonexistent medical attention. Held since February 2, 2005, Abdelkareem Kawas of Jordan states in a letter dated August 7, 2005, addressed to the Civil Rights Division of the U.S. Assistant Attorney General: "In the Lutheran Medical Center I was [scheduled] to see a heart specialist... every two months; since I have been under ICE detention, I have not been able to see a heart doctor for the last six months." He reports that the jail not only refused the heart medication his wife tried to send by mail, but when she tried delivering it to him in person, jail authorities would not accept it. Repeatedly he reports not being referred for a CAT scan despite ongoing chest pain, and when in July a prison doctor finally took a chest X-ray, which revealed a suspicious boil in his lungs, he still had been refused a CAT scan. He reports that he is the sole breadwinner of his family of five and that being held without bail results in great economic hardship for a family that receives no other assistance.

In a Passaic County Jail Inmate Grievance Form dated September 27, 2005, and signed by multiple witnesses, Sami Al-Shahin makes the following complaint: "Last week Lucero Carino Rafael was having heart problems. He was... taken to the hospital [where] he stayed... four days.... After coming back, every morning he was having heart pain and when he complained to the officers they would say he has to hold on and take about an hour before they take him down to the medical clinic. On 9/26/05 [he] was having heart pain again and we told the officer... [After] about a half hour he was taken down to the medical clinic and the nurse told him he was stressing, to jog around, that the pain would go away.

"On the same day me and another inmate spoke to deportation officer Diaz about the incident and Diaz replied that he should just go back to his country. On 9/27/05 around 9:30 A.M. Rafael Carino [collapsed] to the floor.... At first the main problem was getting the [officer's] attention inside the booth. We kept calling him and he didn't respond to us until a lot of inmates came to the bars and started to scream at the officer so he can listen. Then the officer called for the EMT, which came about 30 minutes after Rafael Carino had [collapsed]. Rafael Carino could of died in the time period it took to get the officer's attention and to get the medical help. When inmates surrounded Rafael they thought he had died.... This matter... is very important to us because our lives are involved."

Another inmate grievance form dated September 23, 2005, by Hassan Fagge, who was a diabetic and in twenty-three-hour lockdown, reads: "Yesterday I don't get insulin at night. I want to know why. I take 42 units of insulin every night at 6:30 pm. I was suffering from last night 6:30 pm to 7:27 am this morning, 9/23/05. I am insulin dependent patient. My blood sugar level this morning at 7:42 am was 465g., very high, and my breakfast is 4 slices of bread, juice and oatmeal which is 100% carbohydrate." In a subsequent complaint, dated October 10, 2005, Mr. Fagge includes a chart covering a 20-day period, showing morning, afternoon and night blood sugar readings. Normal readings range from 70 to 109, but from September 21 through October 10, his readings average 249. He writes: "If you look at this diagram my blood sugar level is very high all the time. The jail [is] unable to treat me. No control, no diet, no observation. Anywhere I wrote 'NO,' it means I don't get treatment at [that] time of day." Over the 20-day period the chart reads 'NO' 14 times. The *NJCRDC Voices of the Disappeared* states that, as a result of neglect during the several months of his detention, Fagge has become blind in one eye.

A detainee who goes by the name Amin states in a letter to Blum of December 5, 2005: "These people lock me... in the isolation since 10/2/05... 23 hours [a day].... I still don't get treatment. I'm frozen and I'm sick... sometime my blood pressure goes up to 200.... I'm not a criminal... I'm going to stop taking any medication, insulin, and I will start hunger strike. Because nobody cares about my situation, starving me by giving me very small food."

Detainee Ruth Jean-Baptiste was seriously injured prior to her arrival at Passaic County Jail, when she sustained a fall while washing floors where she was temporarily being held at Metropolitan Detention Center in Brooklyn, New York. Says Blum, "She may have misaligned her spine and injured her coccyx, an injury that can be extremely painful. However there was evidently also an injury causing infection." During her first five months in Passaic County Jail,

Jean-Baptiste writes, "they had me in a punishment cage with no water, no bathroom."

In an undated official complaint, she states: "I arrived in Passaic [County Jail] on July 28, 2004. Since I came I had more than enough reason to beg for deportation." After fourteen months in detention she reports: "My foot bust all by itself. Swollen leg for over 14 months (right leg). The right hip cannot respond to hold my body. The good left hip is acting up now. The right foot is black, dripping water." In another complaint she writes: "Every time I fill out a [grievance] INS refuses all treatments for me. And I get Tylenol for 2 weeks." Still there after fourteen months she writes, "the nurse in charge said there is nothing wrong with me. The only thing I have to do is get up and walk.... How can I trust someone while my pain is unbearable."

On November 1, 2005, sixteen months after her arrival at PCJ, at Blum's instigation, a Dr. Waba agrees to see her. Her report continues: "Dr. Waba yell and scream at me. Very angry. He told me that he is going to take the crutches away from me, and I don't need them because the X-Rays come out negative." Blum adds that "upon release she had an operation where they told her they would have had to amputate had she waited much longer."

Blum describes visiting a woman who was suffering from AIDS. "Her medications were never administered in a regular and timely manner—even though her condition required it. Despite official neglect, the other detainees had been so supportive of her that her spirits remained high. As her condition continued to deteriorate however, the jail administration scheduled her for release. But once released, she succumbed to a depression so severe—with no supportive community around her—that she retreated completely and communicated neither with her sister detainees nor with her lawyer who remained unable to reach her."

According to the *New York Times*, the Organization of American States actually had to intervene asking the United States not to deport Andrea Mortlock, a terminally ill AIDS patient, to Jamaica because it claimed that deportation would violate her basic right to life. In the August 27, 2005, article, the Jamaican government is reported to have refused to issue travel documents on the ground that there was no medical care available to treat AIDS in Jamaica.

PART III

"DHS/ICE Is Breaking Our Families Apart"

Published in *La Bloga*, May 1, 2010

In immigrant detention, scant attention is paid to "family values." A summary of grievances by detainees at Monmouth County Jail dated January 16, 2006, contains the following: "Over 95% of the detainees here are New York based.... All of our families [reside] in New York. DHS/ICE... never in their minds, have they ever taken the hardship for our families to travel over '3 HOURS' (round trip) to see us. What is even [worse] is that the visit is only '15 MINUTES.' And behind bulletproof glass, furthermore, a lot of the detainees are getting deported without being able to even hug or kiss our parents, kids, wife, etc....! [They] are being deported on a daily basis, on an unknown date. [Fifteen] minutes just for them to say 'goodbye' seems really bad! It is just extreme hardship for our families to travel so far for 15 minutes only. DHS/ICE is breaking our families apart before they even try to deport us!"

In a letter to Blum dated June 11, 2005, Roddy Sanchez states: "A lot of times when night falls, I cry because I have a newborn daughter. I got my whole family out here, but when you go in front of the judge they tell you, take your family back to your country, or the judge will say they can always go on welfare...." But the dreams and hopes of most detainees with families do not include taking them back with them to their country of origin, and in many instances, family members are legitimate citizens of the United States.

Quoted in the *NJCRDC Voices of the Disappeared*, in May of 2004 a Sierra Leone journalist in Hudson County Jail writes: "In the event of my deportation, I am afraid that my fiancé and two kids will suffer tremendously, because they depend on me for everything. Who will provide shelter for them? Who will be their role model? Who will be concerned about them going to college? Who will feed them?"

But the display by the presiding authorities of Passaic County Jail of the kinds of casual cruelty that ripped families apart is perhaps best exemplified by two accounts cited here. Although detainees held in "administrative detention" and not classified as criminals, their treatment is comparable to that of ordinary prisoners. Joseph Elchin's letter addressed to Blum of June 2005 states that, despite the repeated pleas of his sister and the initiatives on his behalf by the public defender, he was not allowed to speak to his sister, who wished to notify him that his mother was dying and had been rushed to the hospital to be placed on a ventilator. "As a matter of fact, no one from this institution ever informed me of anything. I [only] learned of the situation when I called home Monday evening."

The Passaic County Sheriff's Department and the jail warden refused him the privilege of visiting his mother on her deathbed before she was removed from the ventilator. "Judge Guzman had denied such a bedside visit stating that 'if I wanted to pay my last respects I could do so at the funeral.'" But in fact, arrangements for him to attend his mother's funeral were denied when, despite intercession by his sister and the public defender, "Judge Guzman refused to sign the order."

The Elchin case, a criminal one, can be compared to a similar case, this one affecting an immigrant detainee. In a letter dated September 26, 2005, addressed to Judge Patricia E. Henry, Juliette Tucker, who is about to be deported to Jamaica, writes: "I have been in the United States for eight years and have never had any criminal involvement. As you know I have three beautiful children who need their mother.... I am pleading not so much for myself, but for my children.... Please take this plea into consideration by allowing me to take all three children with me to Jamaica.... My plan is to go to Jamaica first and shortly after... send for my children.... Due to this, your Honor, I will truly like to see my children before I leave on the 24 October, 2005. Therefore with all humbleness I am seeking your compassion by asking you please, your Honor, allow me a visit with my children. Please, your Honor, I don't want to abandon my children due to... circumstances beyond my control. I am asking you please to grant me one favor to say goodbye and don't take my motherly rights away from me." And although Jean Blum tried to effect an intervention on her behalf, Juliette Tucker was ordered deported without being allowed to see her children.

Deportees are expelled with little more than the shirts on their backs. "Basically they are sent back to a country, not even necessarily their own," Blum explains. "They arrive at the airport of the receiving country with no resources and no means to contact their families." In a letter addressed to her from Kingston, Jamaica, dated August 2, 2005, detainee Barry Walker writes: "When they gave me the flight paper on Friday July 29, they took me straight to the airport with no notice to get any clothes or money together. Somehow I made it home here to my family and I am just breathing a bit of freedom.... Because you are a person among people, I know faith will bring us together again one day."

Prison abuse, physical and verbal, inadequate diet, medical neglect, casual cruelty and disregard of their civil and human rights discourage prisoners from fighting their deportation orders. "Many eventually give up the struggle," says Blum, "but these may be considered the lucky ones." Some—no one knows exactly how many—never get the chance to make that despairing choice.

The Dead, the Disappeared

Still unverified is another kind of Homeland Security list. In his affidavit of December 12, 2005, on behalf of his client's imminent deportation to Syria, Shayana Kadidal cites the case of one 'Abd al-Rahman al-Musa deported from the United States to Syria in January 2005 and who "has not been heard from since." He includes mention of one Nabil al-Marabh, also deported to Syria in 2004, who has "not been heard from again. Amnesty sources indicate that he has been imprisoned and has been tortured."

Although as early as 2007 the *New York Times* had begun drawing attention to immigrant deaths in detention, it was not until April 3, 2009, that it was able to publish an account describing how, in September of 2005, Jean Blum had received a letter addressed to the NJCRDC and copied to ALAFFA reporting the death of one "Ahmed Tender." Written in broken English, nonetheless the message was clear enough: "Today one of the INS immigration die.... No emergency, and the jail very very [careless] about INS detainees. Mr. Ahmed complain about chest pain. Before he die was saying the officer Mr. Ahmed [lie] too much. The officer say Mr. Ahmed to wait.... As Mr. Ahmed arrival in the emergency room he die. So Mr. Ahmed death is need to be investigated... we care very much. Because that can happen to any one of us."

Blum forwarded a copy to the Joint Intake Center of the Department of Homeland Security, where it became the subject of an internal document from the Department of Homeland Security/ICE file dated September 26, 2005, which might never have come to light if the ACLU had not obtained it through a Freedom of Information Act (FOIA) request in 2008, after an in-depth inquiry by the *New York Times*.

The file reads: "Synopsis: On September 20, 2005, the Joint Intake Center (JIC), Washington, D.C., received a packet of correspondence from Ms. Jean Blum, President, American Liberty and Freedom for All (ALAFFA), Paterson, N.J. According to the information received, Mr. Ahmed Tander, a Pakistani detainee housed at the Monmouth County Correctional Institute, died on September 10, 2005, allegedly from a heart attack whose symptoms were obvious, severe and ignored until it was too late."

The death of Ahmad Tanveer (the correct spelling of his name) is of unusual significance because the immigration authorities could produce no record that Mr. Tanveer had ever been detained in the first place, let alone that he had died in their custody. Without the intervention of Jean Blum, this incident might never have come to light. Tom Jawetz of the ACLU reflected on the troubling aspects of this particular case: "We still do not know and we cannot know if there are other deaths that have never been disclosed by ICE or that ICE itself knows nothing about." Congresswoman Zoe Lofgren, pleading the necessity for greater accountability to Congress, wondered if failure to report this death reflected carelessness or "something more sinister."

Said the *Times* (April 3, 2009): "The difficulty of confirming Ahmad [Tanveer]'s very existence showed that death could fall between the cracks in immigration detention, the hundreds of county jails, for-profit prisons and federal detention centers where more than 400,000 people a year are held while the government tries to deport them."

Although deaths in detention were fairly frequent, before 2007, the only documentation available was a list cobbled together by relatives of the deceased or their advocates. As recently as 2007, it included only some twenty names. Through a FOIA request ICE eventually disclosed sixty-two detention deaths since 2004 but declined to provide names, dates, locations, or causes until compelled to do so. By May 5, 2008, the list included 66 names. And by April 3, 2009, it stood at 92. The publication of an article listing the deaths of 2 more detainees, previously unreported, brought the list to 94. A sudden increase of 10 more, as reported by the *New York Times* on August 8, 2009, brought the master list to 104 and then 106, where it stands today.

An examination of the statistical information for 2005 at Passaic County Jail lists seventy-five suicide attempts in that year alone, and one "successful" suicide—number 35 on the ICE master list—which also includes one death "of natural causes," seven deaths by hanging, six cases of asphyxia, one death by drowning (both the latter findings raise a number of questions), and, interestingly, one cause of death (in Corrections Corporation of America's Elizabeth facility), that of Boubacar Bah, which was initially listed as "brain hemorrhage, fractured skull" and is now listed as "undetermined." One death is attributed to electrocution. According to a *New York Times* article dated May 5, 2008, the detainee, Mr. Cesar Gonzalez-Baeza, was operating a jackhammer that hit a power line. Such an unusual cause of death raises an interesting question: what was an immigrant detainee doing operating a jackhammer?

Detainee Gonzalez-Baeza's death (and Ruth Jean-Baptiste's accident while washing floors cited earlier) may have been related to the decades-old practice of leasing out cheap prison labor in American jails and detention centers to private corporations. There have been attempts by Congress—such as the Hawes-Cooper Act (effective 1934) and the Ashurst-Sumners Act (1935), which tried to eliminate prison-plantations and "factories with fences"; but by 1990, with their repeal, it became permissible for prisoners to produce products entering the stream of interstate commerce. According to Andrew Bosworth, an assistant professor of government at the University of Texas at Brownsville, "many of the largest corporations in America have exploited prison labor in what might be called 'Operation Sweatshop.' Starbucks, Microsoft, Boeing, Victoria's Secret and other companies have participated in prison labor programs."

PART IV

A Sputtering Audit

Published in *La Bloga*, May 9, 2010

As far back as 2001, complaints from immigrant detention facilities nationwide started to flood the Department of Homeland Security's inboxes. In response DHS ordered an audit. Although the list of targeted facilities initially stood at 18, after a long delay it was reduced to only 5. The Passaic County Jail under the authority of Sheriff Jerry Speziale was notorious enough to make the final cut. In 2005 94 PCJ detainees turned in complaint sheets indicating alleged areas of mistreatment and abuse. Of these 19 declined to be interviewed. Conceivably the OIG's unwillingness to allow them to talk with a lawyer present may have led to some reluctance. Of the remaining 75, the OIG cherry-picked 32.

But the arrival of what were largely inexperienced auditors in June of 2005 led to mounting recriminations on Sheriff Speziale's part so that by July 2005 he had ordered them out of "his" jail on charges of "arrogance." Summoned to Washington in August, presumably for a reprimand, Speziale returned undaunted, having managed to finesse a new federal contract allowing Passaic County to substitute

U.S. Marshal prisoners for immigrant detainees. At the same rate of seventy-seven dollars a day per prisoner "bed," the Passaic County General Fund would get hardly any time to suffer. The auditors were reinstated in August, and by December the detainees had begun to be removed to other facilities, but an official report from DHS had to wait until November of 2006, when the initial shock of Abu Ghraib had died down.

Shortly after the report's publication, an internal e-mail dated January 19, 2007, by a reporter from the North Jersey News Group queried the DHS: "several former Passaic detainees have called me and said that they told the auditors about abuse, beatings, withholding of food, etc. by jail staffers, but felt those claims weren't reflected in the final audit." Tamara Faulkner of the DHS replied: "We could not develop sufficient evidence to substantiate the credibility of these cases.... For example one detainee stated that he was beaten by the correctional officers and slammed to the floor. We could not find documentary evidence such as medical reports, incident reports, or physical evidence to substantiate the allegation."

Blum was not surprised by the DHS's watered-down report. As far back as June 2005 she had received a letter from detainee Roddy Sanchez stating: "On June 8, 2005 immigration officers from Washington D.C. came to see us.... I thought they're going to stop by and listen to our complaints; instead they said they were coming [back] and they never did."

Blum points out that, far from ending any abuses, shipping the detainees from Passaic to other more distant facilities, some in retaliation for having filed their complaints with the Office of the Inspector General in the first place, occasioned more travel inconvenience for their families and lawyers who needed to visit. It caused Blum to have to curtail her activism because she could no longer afford the detainees' collect long-distance calls on her retiree's income, nor could she be as effective with administrators with whom she had not had reason to develop open channels of communication. And it did not put an end to abuses at Passaic County Jail, where in 2006 the use of dogs was reintroduced.

The Business of Detention Is Business

"When you take to activism, you need to know what you are doing," states Blum. "At the time I joined it, the New Jersey Civil Rights Defense Committee was calling for the release of all immigrants held in administrative detention, but I realized that nothing of the sort was going to happen any time soon.... At 77 dollars a day, nobody gives up that kind of money."

All detention facilities, public and private, enter into a contractual agreement with the Department of Homeland Security/ICE to house detainees. It is in their interest to obtain the most favorable rate per diem and to keep their overhead low. This they accomplish by overcrowding, by providing inadequate diet and poor-to-nonexistent medical attention, and by keeping staff salaries and training to a minimum, resulting in the kinds of prison abuse both verbal and physical, documented earlier. In 2003, at $28,000 per inmate per year plus a 10 percent commissary markup, housing detainees brought in $12 million to the Passaic County Jail, which according to the sheriff's department spokesperson passed directly into the county general fund.

County and federally run jails are now in competition with privately run facilities, of which the numbers rose from five in 1990 to more than two hundred by 2000, But if evidence serves, compared to publicly run facilities, privately operated facilities such as those run by Corrections Corporation of America (with sixty-three facilities in nineteen states) compete to bring their overhead even lower. To secure a profitable bottom line, CCA lobbies a compliant Congress for stricter detention rules; it secures its interests through the use of interlocking directorates, political contributions, and expensive lobbying; to head key projects, it hires retired government administrators and military personnel to guarantee results.

Although it will soon be converted to house only female detainees, CCA's T. Don Hutto facility in Texas, initially billed as "America's family residence," housed women (some of them pregnant), children, and infants in Kevlar tents and required them to wear prison uniforms (even the children). Inmates brought in up to two hundred dollars per inmate per day. The chaplain (who doubles as spokesman for CCA's Houston Processing Center) stated, "We're here to take care of the product they deliver to us. Until they're deported we take care of the detainees as best we can."

In a 2008 conference call to investors from company headquarters in Tennessee, Chief Operations Officer John D. Ferguson got specific about what that care might be. "The intent now is to detain everyone that's apprehended at the border and charge them initially with something called 'entry without inspection.' That will be a misdemeanor, requiring somewhere between 15 and 30 days of detention. So then persons with [a] deportation [order] or minimum conviction, which means someone who ... committed [a] misdemeanor, will face a felony charge, which could lead to six months to two years of detention or incarceration." Enthused by the president's fiscal 2009 budget, he stated, "We see that the budget supports the detention population of 33,000 inmate detainee beds—that's up from 27,500 the previous year and quite above what the ... original budget was. What I am most encouraged about is everything we are hearing says 33,000 is still not enough."

In keeping with the New World Order, the manipulation of language to serve unconstitutional ends is also reflected in the directives of the Office of Detention and Removal (DRO), a subagency of ICE, which calls its ten-year plan "Endgame," an eerie echo of "Final Solution," the term referring to extermination preferred by the Nazi Third Reich. Its goal is removal of all removable aliens by 2012, including 590,000 persons ignoring deportation orders, and 630,000 "criminal" aliens (most of them broken taillight and "entry without inspection" folks), a total of 1.2 million souls. And John D. Ferguson's low-end projections notwithstanding, according to Marjorie Meyers, chief federal defender of south Texas, people convicted of illegal reentry are actually receiving anywhere from four to eight years in jail. "As a result they are pushing undocumented people deeper and deeper underground so they are more exploitable," according to Lisa Brody, a San Benito, Texas, attorney.

Since 2001 Corrections Corporation of America's shares have split twice, multiplied tenfold, closing recently at $24.28. Net profits listed in 2005 annual report of $23.4 million ballooned to $67 million in the first six months of 2009, representing the largest market share of privately run facilities. Its stockholders number government officials including Dick Cheney, who at last count held stock valued at $85 million. Although Corrections Corporation of America ranks first in the percentage of detainee deaths of any public or privately run operator, last available records indicate that CEO Ferguson took home $3 million in 2007 executive compensation.

Holding detainees is not only profitable to government and privately run jails, but it also serves other corporate interests as well. Standing to benefit are telephone companies (prison telephone cards cost ten dollars for the first five minutes), weapons manufacturers, transport and healthcare companies, and food service firms, even hi-tech concerns. Obviating the passé need for tattooed numbers on prisoner forearms, promotional copy for one such corporation reads, "The Quetel Corporation hopes for vigorous sales of its new system to bar code prisoners and equip guards with monitoring scanners."

In the face of ICE's operation "Return to Sender," increasing the arrest quota for its fugitive teams from 125 in 2003 to 1,000 in 2009, Jenni Gainsborough of the ACLU's National Prison Project states the obvious: "[There is a] basic philosophical problem when you begin turning over administration of prisons to people who have an interest in keeping people locked up."

Not the Change We've Waited For

Detainee retention policies are in urgent need of review but as recently as August 2009, the Obama administration declared that it would have to wait until 2010 to overhaul any immigration laws put in place during the Bush years, other than shifting some of its emphasis to holding employers responsible for hiring illegal workers. But a recent federal investigation of American Apparel, a Los Angeles clothing manufacturer, which turned up certain irregularities in the identity documents provided by some workers, resulted in the firing of 1,800 people, presumably driving them deeper into the underground economy.

According to a *New York Times* editorial of October 1, John Morton, the director of Immigration and Customs Enforcement, is quoted, calling it "a milestone in the fight against illegal immigration." "But," questions the *Times*, "one has to ask who benefits from a crackdown like this.... A crackdown that forces 1,800 taxpaying would-be Americans into joblessness in a dismal economy is a law enforcement victory only in the bitterest, narrowest sense. As a solution to the problem of unauthorized workers—1,800 down, millions to go—it's ludicrous."

In October 2009 DHS Secretary Janet Napolitano announced that plans were underway to "improve" the immigrant detention system. The department proposed to consolidate detainees in facilities where conditions would more appropriately reflect their status as noncriminals, it would provide reliable medical care for them, and it would set up a system of more centralized oversight. Still lacking in this proposal, however, are any provisions for enforceable standards governing due process oversight to ensure people are no longer detained without cause, especially over protracted periods of time. Lacking as well is any commitment to developing alternatives to detention, particularly for those with families. And no provision is made for oversight of immigration law enforcement by local police through the 287(g) Program (which deputizes state and local law enforcement agents to catch illegal immigrants) and the "Criminal Alien" laws, which allow local police to collaborate with ICE agents in the harassment of innocent people by such practices as workplace raids, racial profiling, and midnight home raids such as those recently occurring in East Hampton, New York, in clear violation of the Fourth Amendment.

For Jean Blum, a retiree living on a fixed income, during the many months she worked tirelessly to aid detainees, despite the pressure, there must have been something driving her to play David to such a colossal Goliath. "You have phone calls coming day and night. Once the detainees had been moved, I still got calls from Bergen Country or Monmouth County—collect charges I could no longer afford. The authorities [at Monmouth and Bergen] were too far away for me to advocate effectively any longer. Eventually you burn out. But I am very much aware of the issues involving people who are displaced. I could not turn my back because that is my own history as a Holocaust survivor but love has little to do with it," she says. "I am not conscious of harboring feelings of love."

Asked to comment about Napolitano's recently proposed reforms, she is uncompromising. "Comment? Are you kidding? Throw all the bums out and start over again. Except there are no different bums to take over the reins! Things were better under [the Bush administration]. Lawlessness was the order of the day and there was no doubt about that. After [Bush] the deluge is where we are now."

Note: During the course of his presidency, Barack Obama oversaw the deportation of 2.7 million people, or about 1,000 immigrants a day. Today, the 34,000 ICE beds per day mandated by Congress are expected to increase to 40,000 beds per day under the present Trump administration.

ABOUT THE AUTHOR

Cecile Pineda is the author of six published novels: *Face*, which won the Gold Medal from the Commonwealth Club of California, the First Fiction Award from the American Academy of Arts and Letters, a National Book Award nomination, and a 2014 Neustadt Prize nomination for international fiction; *The Love Queen of the Amazon*, written with the assistance of an NEA Fiction Fellowship and named Notable Book of the Year by the *New York Times*; *Frieze*, set in ninth-century India and Java, a meditation that pits the power of the state against the slow resistances of human life; *Fishlight: a Dream of Childhood*; *Bardo99*, a mononovel that speaks in the voice of the twentieth century; and *Redoubt*, a meditation on gender. She has published three works of nonfiction, *Devil's Tango: How I Learned the Fukushima Step by Step*, a criminal exposé of the nuclear industry; *Apology to a Whale: Words to Mend a World*, an exploration of language at the intersection of archeology and comparative linguistics as the root of the world's present power alignments; and *Three Tides: Writing at the Edge of Being*, a memoir highlighting the experience of Hurricane Katrina. All works remain in print.

Pineda's archive forms part of the Special Collections Library of Stanford University. Of her fiction, J. M. Coetzee has written: "Cecile Pineda is a novelist of the utmost artistic integrity."

Before her work as a writer, Pineda founded and directed Theatre of Man, her own experimental theater company. Visit her web page at cecilepineda.com.

Other works by Cecile Pineda

    Face

    Frieze

    The Love Queen of the Amazon

    Fishlight

    Bardo 99

    Redoubt

    Devil's Tango: How I Learned the Fukushima Step by Step

    Apology to a Whale: Words to Mend a World

    Three Tides

CRUX, THE GEORGIA SERIES IN LITERARY NONFICTION

Debra Monroe, *My Unsentimental Education*

Sonja Livingston, *Ladies Night at the Dreamland*

Jericho Parms, *Lost Wax: Essays*

Priscilla Long, *Fire and Stone: Where Do We Come From? What Are We? Where Are We Going?*

Sarah Gorham, *Alpine Apprentice*

Tracy Daugherty, *Let Us Build Us a City*

Brian Doyle, *Hoop: A Basketball Life in Ninety-Five Essays*

Michael Martone, *Brooding: Arias, Choruses, Lullabies, Follies, Dirges, and a Duet*

Andrew Menard, *Learning from Thoreau*

Dustin Parsons, *Exploded View: Essays on Fatherhood, with Diagrams*

Clinton Crockett Peters, *Pandora's Garden: Kudzu, Cockroaches, and Other Misfits of Ecology*

André Joseph Gallant, *A High Low Tide: The Revival of a Southern Oyster*

Justin Gardiner, *Beneath the Shadow: Legacy and Longing in the Antarctic*

Emily Arnason Casey, *Made Holy: Essays*

Sejal Shah, *This Is One Way to Dance: Essays*

Lee Gutkind, *My Last Eight Thousand Days: An American Male in His Seventies*

Cecile Pineda, *Entry Without Inspection: A Writer's Life in El Norte*

www.ingramcontent.com/pod-product-compliance
Lightning Source LLC
Chambersburg PA
CBHW010927180426
43192CB00043B/2784